Traditional or contemporary, religious, family or famous, this book will help you find the perfect name for your baby . . .

◊ **CECILÍA** is the patron saint of musicians
◊ **VIDAL** means life
◊ **BERNARDO** means strong as a bear
◊ **MARGARITA** means pearl
◊ **FELIPO** is a lover of horses
◊ **GLORIA** means fame and glory

¿Cómo te llamas, Baby?
THE HISPANIC BABY NAME BOOK

THE HISPANIC BABY NAME BOOK

¿Cómo te llamas, Baby?

JAMIE MARTINEZ WOOD

BERKLEY BOOKS, NEW YORK

¿CÓMO TE LLAMAS, BABY?

A Berkley Book / published by arrangement with
the author

PRINTING HISTORY
Berkley edition / May 2001

The Penguin Putnam Inc. World Wide Web site address is
www.penguinputnam.com

ISBN: 0-425-17959-1

BERKLEY®
Berkley Books are published by The Berkley Publishing Group,
a division of Penguin Putnam Inc., 375 Hudson Street,
New York, New York 10014.
BERKLEY and the "B" design
are trademarks belonging to Penguin Putnam Inc.

PRINTED IN THE UNITED STATES OF AMERICA

10 9 8 7 6 5 4 3 2 1

CONTENTS

Acknowledgments

I want to profusely thank Laura Hernandez, Pedro Carbajal, and Katie Weyermann from the bottom of my heart for all their hard work and dedication to this project. I also want to thank my editor, Christine Zika, and agent, Julie Castiglia, for their support.

Foreword

Parents can often spend months searching for just the right name for their baby. This journey can be joyful, frustrating, and oftentimes fraught with indecision. The naming of a child is not something to be taken lightly. Many of us have memories of seeing a child teased and taunted because of their name. So it is with great care and love that parents search for that perfect fit.

I was not an exception. When I found out I was pregnant I pored over baby name books and listened intently to TV, radio, and conversations, hoping to find a name that would click. But my mind was also very preoccupied because my mother was extremely ill. Yet I never doubted that she would be all right. How could anything possibly happen to her? This was to be her first grandchild. She was so excited and anticipated holding this precious bundle in her arms.

Then like an electrical jolt, I received the news that she was dead. I was eight months pregnant. Grief held me in her clutches. The only thing that momentarily brought me out of this despair was the thought of bringing life into this world. The person that I adored and loved had been so cruelly taken from me. The void was unbearable.

A month later, still in a haze, I gave birth to a beautiful baby girl. Somewhere deep inside of me I struggled to find a shred of joy. The joy I needed so desperately to give to my daughter. Mentally I reviewed my list of baby names. I needed a name that symbolized the happiness that was so lacking in my life.

Until I remembered a time of innocence and light. Flashes of my six-year-old best friend, Jamie, came to my mind. She was the embodiment of sunshine and laughter. Together we created mud-pie masterpieces and were tight-rope walkers balancing precariously on our backyard fence. Her spirit of adventure was evident in all she did. Her laughter was infectious and she was a daredevil to the first degree. She made me smile. So I bestowed this name on my daughter, hoping that she would inherit these qualities.

And of course, her middle name would be Della, after my mother. Although she would never see her grand-mother, her nana, she would always have this incredible link with her. They would share a name; a name that sym-bolized a strong, proud Hispanic woman, a fifth-generation Californio; a woman who fought for injustices and treated everyone with compassion and love. I knew that by gracing her with this name, my daughter would have a most beau-tiful and protective angel to watch over her all her life.

Every baby's name has a story, and particularly Latino babies' names are often tied with the heartstrings of emo-tions.

—CATHI MARTINEZ,
mother of the author

Thou hast turned for me my mourning into dancing.
Psalms 30:11

Author's Note

My name represents two things: my individualism and my connection to a structure much bigger than myself. Jamie is the supplanter, which means "to replace." When my mother named me thus, I was being asked to replace sorrow with joy. Yet in return the mirror image that was shown to me—the symbol of my name from my mother's perspective—was the essence of childlike wonder, enthusiasm, faith, and adventure. The name we give our children represents the family. Not demanding but imploring the child to respond to this call and fulfill the destiny inherent in the meaning of their name. It was my honor to help my family, and one I gladly took on, for in return I received the unyielding support of a Latino family. I became my name.

Although the saint information has been verified with several sources, it does not represent a complete collection or all interpretations.

Names Derived from
Saints

FROM THE EARLY days in the Catholic Church saints have acted as advocates between God and humankind. They have worked miracles and been a source of protection and great comfort. The term *saint* originates from the Latin word *sanctus,* meaning hallowed or consecrated. Those who have earned sainthood have demonstrated Christlike faith, holiness, and devotion to God and his love in their willingness to die for their cause. It is believed that death begins life in heaven. Saints ascend to heaven and begin a blessed and comforted life. On the day of their death we pay homage to these sacred martyrs and celebrate their freedom and bliss in living with God with a feast day. Often children are named after the saint whose feast day is the day they are born. In this way they can call upon their patron saint for guidance and protection as they already have a connection with this martyr.

In addition, saints have special roles as patrons or guardians and defenders of places and people. It is in this arena that they work their miracles. The list of patronages includes such subjects as women, children, indoor professions, outdoor pursuits, personal fears and problems, health, arts and crafts, the animal kingdom, crises and dangers. To name a child after a saint confers upon the child the special protection of this holy saint.

There are many saints listed in the Roman martyrology. A complete list of saints with Hispanic names can be found on pages 149–161. Here you will find the saints are listed by feast day for easy reference to your child's birthday. The following list is a more comprehensive compilation of the most popular and well-known saints as well as their patronage and emblems they are usually depicted with.

Saint's Name	Patronage	Emblem	Feast Day
Ágata (f)	Breast disorders	Breasts	February 5
Alberto	Scientific and medical research	Books	November 15
Alejo	Humility, sons	Surrounded by beggars	July 17
Aloisio (m)	Teenager boys and people with kidney problems	Himself as a teenager	June 21
St. Aloisio Gonzaga	Masons and sculptures	Fleur de lys, dove, crown and scepter tipped with the hand of God	August 25
Ambrosio (m)	Bees	Beehives	December 7
Ana (f)	Pregnancy, housewives, cabinet makers, grandmothers	An angel, flowering rod, crown, nest of birds, Mary in a cradle	July 26
Andrés (m)	Fishermen, sailors, single women	Two fishes, fishhook, fishing net, X-shaped cross	November 30

Saint's Name	Patronage	Emblem	Feast Day
Angela	Universities and women	Herself with a little girl	January 27
Antonio	Butchers, grave diggers, basket and brush makers	pig, goat, two lions, Tau cross (T), bell	January 17
Antonio de Padera	Lost property, good harvest	Christ child, a chest with a heart, fish, book, lily	June 13
Augustín	Theologians, brewers, printers	Pastoral staff, heart of fire	August 28
Barbara	Lightning, thunderstorms, miners, gunners	Tower, palm, cannon, chalice	December 4
Bartolomé	Tanners, cheese merchants	Tanner's knife, scimitar, three knives, the devil under his feet, St. Mateo's gospel	August 24
Benito	Schoolchildren, the dying, farmworkers, coppersmiths	Ball of fire; a raven and pitcher; briars and roses; broken cup with serpent on book; monastery on a mountain	February 11
Bernabé	Harvesters	Dalmatic (special vest worn by a deacon at Mass), three stones, a hatchet	June 11
Bernardo of Clairvaux	Beekeepers, honey and candle makers	Beehive, pen and ink, chained devil	August 20

Saint's Name	Patronage	Emblem	Feast Day
Bernardo of Montjoux	Skiers and mountaineers	Snow-capped mountains and Saint Bernard dogs	May 28
Bibiana	Headaches	Branch and pillar	December 2
Blas	Wild animals, wool combers	Wool comb, two crossed candles	February 3
Brigida	Scholars, inspiration, fire, Ireland	Well, fire, smith-crafting, spear	July 22
Bruno	Victims of demonic possession	Flowering crucifix, star on his chest, seven stars	October 11
Camilo	Nurses, disease, the sick, hospital	Patients in sick room	July 14
Carlos	Sunday school teachers, ordinands and seminarians	The word *humilitus* (humility) with a cross; orb and cross	November 4
Catalina de Alejandra	Millers, young girls, nurses, philosophers, the dying, spinners	Spiked wheel	November 25
Catalina de Siena	Protection from fire	Heart, lily, stigmata, cross	April 30
Cayetano	Poetry		August 7
Cecilía	Musicians	Organ, lute, two wreaths of roses and lilies, harp	November 22
Ciprano	Authors	Book	September 16

Saint's Name	Patronage	Emblem	Feast Day
Clara de Asís	Television, embroiderers, those with eye troubles	Chalice and host; a tall cross; lily; monstrance; ciborium	August 11
Clemente	Lighthouse, stonecutters, blacksmiths	Fountains; anchor; tiara; maniple; marble temple at sea	November 23
Cosme y Damian	Doctors, surgeons, barbers, pharmacists, hairdressers, dentists	Box of ointments, phial, and jars; arrows; rod of Aesculapius (Roman god of medicine and healing)	September 27
Cristina	Psychic abilities	Angels holding a string attached to her dress	July 24 and December 15
Cristóforo	Safe travel; surfers; those in danger of water, storms, or sudden death	Christ child on his shoulder; lantern; palm tree; river	July 28
David	Wales	Cross and staff	March 1 and December 29
Domingo	Astronomy, friars, preachers	Lily; greyhound; book; star on his forehead; dog holding a torch	May 12
Dortea	Florists and gardeners	Angel with basket of apples or roses; sword; crown	February 6
Elena	Archaeologists	Crown; cross; hammer and nails; open book and crown	August 18

Saint's Name	Patronage	Emblem	Feast Day
Elisabeth	Pregnant women	Elizabeth greeting Mary or holding John the Baptist	November 5
Eloy	Jewelers, blacksmiths, goldsmiths	Horseshoe, hammer, and pincers	December 1
Enrique			July 15
Esteban	Stonemasons, builders, horses	Dalmatic (tunic worn by deacon); three stones; stones in a napkin; stones on a book	December 26
Eugenio	Music and poetry	Singing	November 13
Eusebio		Gospels	August 2 and December 16
Felipe	Orators	Mother angel and cherubs	May 26
Fernando	Engineers, rulers, governors, magistrates, the poor, prisoners	Greyhound	May 30
Filomena	Virgins	Arrows, a palm, flower	August 10
Francis de Asís	Ecologists, animals, birds, Green movement	Birds; deer; winged crucifix with five rays; stigmata; crown of thorns; lighted lamp; fine clothes and bag of gold at his feet	October 4

Saint's Name	Patronage	Emblem	Feast Day
Gabriel	Diplomats, telecommunications, televisions, radio, postal services, stamp collectors, women in childbirth	Spear, shield, lily	March 24
Genevève	Disasters	Candles, bread, herds of sheep, keys	January 3
Geronimo	Librarians and scholars	Lion, inkhorn and pen, fox, hare, partridge, open Bible, fawn	September 30
Gertrudis		Staff, sacred heart of Jesus	November 16
Gregorio the Great	Singers, music, popes, schools	Crozier; dove; tiara; altar; an ancient manuscript	September 3 or March 12
Gregorio the Wondermaker	Earthquakes	Catastrophic scene	November 17
Guillermo		Pallium	June 8
Hilario	Slow learners, the mentally ill, lawyers	Child in cradle, trumpet, serpent on a stick	January 13
Honoria			
Hugo	Swan	Swan	April 1 or November 17
Ignacio de Antioch	Sore throats	Lions, chains	October 17

Saint's Name	Patronage	Emblem	Feast Day
Ignacio de Loyola	Missionaries and universities	Preaching to the people with his followers of the Society of Jesus dressed in black	July 31
Ines	Young girls, virgins, or Girl Guides	Lamb, dove holding a ring, sword	January 21
Isabel	War	Rose, beggar	July 4
Isidro	Farmers and Madrid	Angels, corn	May 15
Jorge	Soldiers, especially cavalry; riders; knights; Boy Scouts; armoires, butchers	Amour, a dead dragon, broken wheel, white flag with a red cross	April 23
Jose	Fatherhood, family, bursars, engineers, house hunters, manual workers, carpenters	Carpenter's square	March 19
Juan de la Cruz			November 24

Saint's Name	Patronage	Emblem	Feast Day
Juan the Baptist	Motorways, leather and wool workers, road construction workers	Camel-hair tunic; locust; his head on a platter; lamb; lamb on a book with seven seals; open Bible; scroll with the words *Ecce Agnus Dei* (Behold the Lamb of God)	June 24 and August 29
Juan the Evangelist	Writers	Cup and serpent, eagle, serpent on a scroll, scroll of his gospel	December 27
Julián	Publicans, boatman, travelers	Hart, oar	February 12
Justo	Philosophers		August 4
Leonardo de Noblac	Imprisonment, childbirth, prisoners of war	Chains, fetters with manacles	November 6
Lorenzo	Cooks, brewers, confectioners, armorers, students, washerwomen, glaziers, librarians, poor people	Gridiron, purse or plate of money, dalmatic, thurible or censer	August 10
Lucia	Blindness, glaziers, cutlers, those with eye trouble, those who work with lights	Two eyes on a platter; sword; lamp; three crowns; two oxen; a cup; dagger; ropes	December 13

Saint's Name	Patronage	Emblem	Feast Day
Marcelo			October 30
Marcos	Lions, cattle farmers, lawyers, glaziers	Winged lion; a pen; a book and scroll; scroll with the words *Pax tibi* (Peace be to you)	April 25
Margarita			July 20
Maria Magdalena	Penitents, perfumers, hairdressers, glovers, contemplatives	Fine clothes and loose hair; pot of ointment; skull; vase; crucifix	July 22
Marta	Housewives, innkeepers, cooks, servants, lay sisters, waiters, dietitians	Keys at her waist; broom; ladle; cooking pots; dragon bound with a girdle; water pot and asperge	July 29
Martín	Racial harmony; social justice; public education; beggars; soldiers, especially cavalry; riders	Horse; sword and cloak cut in half; goose; scourge; hare; broken idols' chair in flames; demon at his feet	November 11
Mateo	Accountants, tax collectors, customs officers, security guards	Pen and inkwell; spear; winged man; dolphin; sword or halberd; money bag, money box, or chest; carpenter's square; axe; stones; scroll of his gospel	September 21

Saint's Name	Patronage	Emblem	Feast Day
Matilde	Poor people	Church and crucifix; altar; money bag	March 14
Maurico	Weavers, dyers, soldiers	Battle scene	September 22
Miguel	Grocers, battle, security forces	Scales, dragon, sword, man in full armor with huge wings holding a shield and scales	September 29
Mónica	Wives, mothers	Girdle, tears, book, staff, monstrance, veil or hankie	August 27
Nicolás	Children (especially boys), sailors, merchants, pawnbrokers, churches, apothecaries	Three balls; three golden apples on a book; anchor; ship; three purses; three loaves; Trinity symbol on a cope (ceremonial cloak)	December 6
Oportuna	Benedictine order	Veil	April 22
Pablo	Those with snakebites; upholsterers; tentmakers (his own trade)	Sword; book; serpent and fire; palm tree; phoenix; three fountains; scrolls with the names of his epistles	June 30
Pancracio	Cramps, headaches, children	Palm, sword, stone	May 12

Saint's Name	Patronage	Emblem	Feast Day
Panteleón	Medicine	Middle finger and thumb in shape of an "O"; a silver statue and dried blood caked on a phial	July 27
Pasqual	Eucharistic congresses and fraternities of the blessed sacrament	Garbed as a Franciscan friar	May 17
Paula	Widows	Instruments of passion; book and staff; sponge; scourge	January 26
Pedro	Longevity, the church, the papacy, fishermen, boat builders, clock makers	Two crossed keys; book; crowing cock; a fish; two swords; shepherd's staff and two keys	June 29
Pedro Alcántara	Night watchmen, sleep	Quill and book	October 19
Ricardo	Coach drivers	Plow; book and staff; chalice at his feet	April 3
Roberto	Ecclesiastical lawyers and catechists	Book, inkwell, pen	September 17 and May 13
Rosa de Lima	Florists, gardeners	Crown of roses with thorns; the holy infant; needle and thimble; spiked crown	August 30
Salvador	Feet	Barefoot	March 18

Saint's Name	Patronage	Emblem	Feast Day
Santiago	The dying	Windmill, halberd, three stones, bread	June 4
Santiago de Mayor (James the Great)	Rheumatism, soldiers, cavalry, veterans, furriers	Cockleshell; pilgrim's staff; hat; cloak; wallet and purse; keys; white horse and white flag	July 25
Sebastian	Archers, athletes, soldiers	Arrows, crown	January 20
Silvestre	Baptism, leprosy	Chained dragon (or bull) and atiara; the principle scene is the baptism of Constantine	December 31
Simon y Judas	Lost causes	Fish and book; anchor and oar; fuller's bat	October 28
Teresa	Spain	Roses and lilies; heart in flames; dove; flaming arrows	October 15
Tomás	Architects, builders, carpenters, masons, surveyors	Spear and lance; carpenter's square and lance; builder's rule; five wounds of Christ; book and spear; Virgin Mary's girdle	July 3
Tomás Aquinas	Academics, booksellers, philosophers, theologians, pencil makers	Star; chalice; ox; monstrance	January 28
Úrsula	Teacher of girls	Arrows, clock, ship	October 21
Valentín	Love, medicine, doctors	Administering to the sick, birds	February 14

Saint's Name	Patronage	Emblem	Feast Day
Venceslao	Czechoslovakia	Armor and shield with an engraved eagle	September 28
Verónica	Laundry workers	Christ's face printed on a veil	July 9
Vincente	All charities, hospitals, prisons	Orphanage or hospital, child in his arms	January 22
Vito	Dancers, actors, comedians	Performance scene	June 15
Zita	Domestic servants	Home life	April 27

Names Related to the
Church

THE LATINO CULTURE is steeped in mysticism. When we decide on a name for our children it is as if we tenderly take them from God's arms in heaven and ground them in our human world, this earthly plane. The role of the church is ensconced into daily activities and of course special events. So ingrained is religion into the Latino belief system and frame of reference that children are often named after the holiness and miracles of church-related events and objects.

By naming our children after sacrosanct rituals, objects, and festivals associated with the church we demonstrate to our children that faith and belief in the holiness reside within us and all around us. This gives them a solid grounding to begin their spiritual life. Naming a baby after something sacred is the parents' way of expressing the hope that their child will develop or aspire to the spiritual quality inherent in their name. In addition to registering the child under the protection of God and the church, this is an underlying premise for the baptism: as we call the child by his or her name it's as if we call them into existence.

Name	Symbolism
Abdallah (m)	Servant of God
Abdías (m)	Slave of God
Abdiel (m)	Servant of God
Abdón (m)	Servant of God
Abimael (m)	Father of God
Adeodato (m)	One given to God
Ananías (m)	God is merciful
Angel(a) (m/f)	Messenger of God
Ansberto (m)	Splendor of God
Anselmo (m)	God is protection
Anunciación (m/f)	Refers to the time the angel Gabriel announced to Mary her pregnancy and upcoming birth of the Son of God
Aparación (m/f)	Refers to Jesus' appearance after resurrection
Asunción (m/f)	Refers to the popular or inevitable assumption that Mary would ascend to heaven
Atanasio(a) (m/f)	Spiritual immortality
Baptisto(a) (m/f)	One who baptizes
Celestino(a) (m/f)	Belonging to Heaven
Ciríraco	Belonging to the Lord
Concepción (f)	Refers to the Immaculate Conception
Conseja (f)	Good Counsel of the Virgin María
Corazon (f)	Refers to Sacred Heart of Jesus Christ
Crisóforo (m)	Bearing Christ
Cristían (m)	A follower of Christ
Cristo (m)	To anoint
Cruz(a) (m/f)	Cross, crucifix
Daniel(a) (m/f)	God is my judge
Deogracias (m)	Thanks to God

Name	Symbolism
Domingo(a) (m/f)	Belonging to the Lord
Dorotea (f)	Gift of God
Dositeo (m)	Gift of God
Eleázar (m)	God has helped
Elías (m)	Jehovah is God
Eliezar (m)	God is my help
Elisabeth (f)	God is my oath
Eliseo (m)	God is salvation
Encarnacíon (f)	Refers to Christ as the human incarnation of God
Engracia (f)	By the grace of God
Epifanio(a) (m/f)	Refers to Epiphany, a Christian festival that commemorates three events: the visit of the Three Wise Men, Jesus' baptism, and Jesus' first public miracle
Epirita (f)	Holy Spirit
Evangelina (f)	Refers to the four evangelists: Mateo, Marcus, Lucas, and Juan, a.k.a. Matthew, Mark, Luke, and John
Exaltación (m)	Refers to miraculous removal of Christ's cross
Ezequías (m)	God strengthens
Ezquiel (m)	God strengthens
Febronio (m)	February, refers to La Purificación de Nuestra Señora
Fuensanta (f)	Holy Source
Gabriel(la) (m/f)	God is my strength, also the name of the angel who appeared to Mary and told her of her upcoming pregnancy
Godeliva (f)	God's gift
Isabel (f)	God is my oath

Name	Symbolism
Isaiah (m)	God is my salvation
Ismael (m)	God hears
Israel (m)	Contender with God
Jeremías (m)	God will uplift
Jesús (m)	Son of God, God is salvation
Joaquín (m)	God will establish
José(fa) (m/f)	God shall add
Josefat (m)	He who has God as his judge
Juan(a) (m/f)	God is gracious
Judas (m)	Praise of God
Lázaro (m)	God has helped
Luz (f)	Our Lady of Light
Malaquias (f)	Angel, messenger
Manuel(a) (m/f)	God is with us
María (m)	Virgin Mother
Mateo (m)	Gift of God
Mercedes (f)	Our Lady of Mercy
Miguel(a) (m/f)	He who is like God, also angel responsible for carrying out God's judgment
Milagros (f)	Our Lady of Miracles
Mireya (f)	God has spoken
Natalia (f)	Natal Day, Christmas
Nathaniel (m)	Gift of God
Navidad (f)	Christ's birth
Osmundo (m)	Divine protection
Osvaldo (m)	Power of God
Pascual(a) (m/f)	Refers to Easter
Piedad (f)	Our Lady of Piety
Preciosa (f)	Precious blood of Christ

Name	Symbolism
Presencia (f)	Refers to God's omnipresence and the presence of Christ in the Eucharist
Presentación (f)	Refers to the presentation of Christ
Purificacíon (f)	Refers to the ritual purification of Mary after Christ's birth
Querbín	Cherub
Rafael(a) (m/f)	God has healed
Refugio (m/f)	Our Lady of Safe Haven
Remedio (m/f)	Our Lady of Remedies
Rosario (f)	Rosary
Sacramento (m)	Sacrament, sacred
Samjuana (f)	God is gracious
Samuel (m)	Name of God
Sancho (m)	Sacred
Santa (f)	Saint
Simón (m)	God has heard
Socorro (f)	Our Lady of Perpetual Help
Soledad (f)	Our Lady of Solitude
Teodoro(a) (m/f)	God's gift
Teodosio (m)	Like a gift of God
Teófilo (m)	Beloved of God
Timoteo (m)	Honor, respect God
Tobias (m)	God is good
Tránsito(a) (m/f)	Refers to transfer of the Virgin María from earth to heaven
Trinidad (m)	Trinity, three persons of God
Tristán	He who is God
Zacarías	Remembrance of God

Nature Names

LATINOS HOLD A strong link to their native roots. Their indigenous ancestors had a deep spiritual connection to nature. Indians of all nations survived by living in harmony with their natural surroundings. They followed the changing seasons with ritual and reverence. Nature was woven into the fabric of their lives. As Latinos we have taken inspiration from our ancestors in innumerable ways. For example, many names for our children come from nature. Sometimes the name itself has a direct translation into the everyday language. Other times the names in this category derive from Latin words. These names represent the flora and fauna, the animal kingdom, and the elements of earth itself.

Name	Translation
Abejundio (m)	Bee
Acacio (m)	Acacia tree
Aciano (m)	Blue-bottle flower
Acilino (m)	Eagle
Adán (m)	Red earth

Name	Translation
Alameda (f)	Cottonwood grove
Alaqua (f)	Sweet gum tree
Anatolio(a) (m/f)	Sunrise
Apolo (m)	Of the sun's power
Apolonio(a) (m/f)	Light from the sun
Aponi (f)	Butterfly
Arno (m)	Eagle
Arnoldo (m)	Powerful as an eagle
Arnulfo (m)	Eagle and wolf
Aurelio(a) (m/f)	Gold
Avanta (f)	Turtle
Avellino(a) (m/f)	Place of hazelnuts
Avendela (f)	Dawn
Avenita (f)	Fawn
Azalia (f)	Flower
Azuncena (f)	White lily
Beliarosa (f)	Beautiful rose
Berilo (m)	Sea-green gem
Bernardo (m)	Strong as a bear
Bertrán (m)	Bright raven
Cabalina (f)	Horse
Camelio(a) (m/f)	Flower
Caparina (f)	Type of butterfly
Celadonia (f)	Swallow
Celina (f)	Light of the moon
Chenoa (f)	White dove
Chimalis (f)	Bluebird
Cholena (f)	Bird
Cirilo (m)	Sun
Cosme (m)	Cosmos, universe

Name	Translation
Crisanto (m)	Chrysanthemum
Dahlia (f)	Flower
Débora (f)	Bee
Delfina (f)	Dolphin
Eberardo (m)	Strong as a boar
Esmeralda (f)	Emerald
Estella (f)	Star
Ester (f)	Star
Fabio (m)	Bean
Fabiola (f)	Bean
Febe (f)	Light of the moon
Felipe(a) (m/f)	Lover of horses
García (m)	Fox
Helio (m)	Sun
Hortencia (f)	Gardener
Ignacio (m)	Fire
Iris (f)	Rainbow
Jacaranda (f)	Flower
Jacinto (m)	Hyacinth
Jano (m)	Brilliant as the sun
Jazmín (f)	Jasmine, a fragrant plant
Jemsa (f)	Gem, precious stone
Jonas (m)	Gentle as a dove
Jorge (m)	Earthworker, farmer
Larrina (f)	Laurel
Laurentia (f)	Laurel
Lauro(a) (m/f)	Laurel
Leandro (m)	Lion man
Léon (m)	Lion
Leonardo (m)	Lion bold

Name	Translation
Leoncio(a) (m/f)	Lion
Leopardo (m)	Leopard
Lobo (m)	Wolf
Lorenzo (m)	Laurel
Lilia (f)	Lily
Margarita (f)	Pearl
Marino(a) (m/f)	A man of the sea
Melisa (f)	Bee
Nereida (f)	Sea nymph
Nevar (f)	To snow
Nieves (f)	Snow
Olivia (f)	Olive tree
Paloma (f)	Dove
Pedro (m)	Rock
Pentea (f)	Flower from the orchid family
Petronila (f)	Rock
Raquel (f)	Ewe, sheep
Raul (m)	Wolf counsel
Rodolfo (m)	Famous wolf
Rosa (f)	Rose
Seferino(a) (m/f)	Zephyr, west wind
Silvano(a) (m/f)	Forest, a wood
Silvia (f)	Forest, a wood
Solana (f)	Sunshine
Susana (f)	Lily
Tabita (f)	Gazelle
Úrsula (f)	Little she-bear
Viola (f)	Violet
Xochil (f)	Where flowers abound
Yolanda (f)	Violet

Family Names

To be worthy of honor and maintain this respect is an important achievement within the Latino community. This dignity often comes from a family name. Through our family names we can trace back to our ancestors and take pride in their determination, courage, and valor. We can call upon their strength for our trials and tribulations and know someone has paved a path before us to make our road a little less bumpy.

While many surnames originate from one's occupation, where one lives, his appearance, or characteristics, others found their roots from other sources. In the Middle Ages, it was customary to have a surname that had derived from your father's first name. To honor the lineage of the child's maternal ancestors, parents often included the mother's maiden name in the child's full name.

Often Latino children are named after beloved predecessors. This tradition, which can often be traced for many generations, may involve giving the child a grandparent or parent's name for a first or middle name. Often the use of suffixes such as *ito, cita, ila,* or *ina* form a diminutive and distinguish between father and son or grandmother and granddaughter.

The list of pet names, also known as diminutives, can be endless, and often quite distinctive depending upon the parents' imagination. For this reason we have listed only the most popular diminutives after each name. The same follows suit for unique spellings and alternate variations of names.

Girls' Names A-Z

Aarona *(ah roan' nah)* Hebrew origin. Feminine version of Aarón. Derived from *ahrōn* (exalted). Alternative sources offer teaching or singing as the meaning for this name.

Abegaíl *(ah bee gah eel')* Hebrew origin. Derived from *avīgayil* (father's joy). In the Bible, she was King David's wife and queen. Variation: Abigail.

Abila *(ah bee' lah)* Latin origin. Derived from Abella (the beautiful) a name that has its roots in *bella* (beautiful).

Abril *(ah breel')* Etruscan origin. Related to the Latin word *aprilis* (open). The fourth month of the calendar year also gets its name from the same root word. It marks the spring season when flowers are blooming and opening up to the sun and its warmth.

Ada *(ah dah)* Hebrew origin. The name means ornament. Variation: Adina.

Adela *(ah day' lay)* German origin. Derived from *adal* (noble). Variations: Adelene, Adelina, Della.

Adelaida *(ah day lie' da)* German origin. The name combines the elements *adal* (noble) and *heid* (kind, class): hence the name means of noble birth or special class or condition. She was a tenth-century German empress. Her feast day is December 16. Diminutives:

Layda, Lina, Yaya. Variations: Adela, Adelaria, Adeleita, Delaida.

Adelinda *(ah day leen' dah)* German and Spanish origin. Derived from the composition of *adal* (noble) and *linda* (pretty): hence the name means the pretty noble girl, or beautiful courtesan. The adjectives *adored* and *gentle* are also attributed to this name. Variations: Adalilia, Audilia.

Adeltrudis *(ah dayl true' dees)* German origin. The name is a combination of *adal* (of noble birth) and *trut* (dear, kind, loving): hence the combination means beloved of the nobility.

Adelvisa *(ah dayl bee' sah)* German origin. The name combines the elements of *adal* (noble birth) with *wis* (sabio, expert): hence the arrangement means *sabio en la nobleza*, meaning wise person of the nobility.

Adoración *(ah doe ray' see own)* Latin origin. The name means adoration and refers to the love for Jesus Christ.

Adriana *(ahd ree ah' nah)* Latin origin. Feminine version of Adrián. Derived from the Latin surname of Adriānus (man from the city of Adria). Variation: Adría.

Ágata *(ah' gah tah)* Greek origin. The name means compassionate, good. A third-century saint maintained a strong conviction to stay a virgin, chaste and pure. Despite the many cruelties she was subjected to, she kept her faith. The name is also related to the stone agate, which is used to balance the male and female aspects within oneself. It is also believed to transform negative energy and increase perceptiveness. Variations: Agadita, Ayguda.

Agraciana *(ah grah tsee ahn' nah)* Spanish origin. The name means to forgive or to pardon.

Agueda *(ah gway' dah)* German origin. The name means good, pleasant, worthy.

Aída *(ah ee' dah)* Uncertain origin. She was the heroine of a nineteenth-century opera by Verdi. Diminutive: Ducha. Variations: Ahida, Ayda.

Aislara *(ay slar' rah)* Spanish origin. The name means to separate. It has also come to describe one who likes the freedom in solitude.

Alalita *(ah lah lee' tah)* Borrowed from a stone found in Italy.

Alameda *(ah lah meh' dah)* Native American origin. The name means cottonwood grove. Cottonwoods grew abundantly in southern California at the time of the ranchero period. Their shade was sought by the riverside during the hot Indian summers.

Alaqua *(ah lah' quah)* Native American origin. The name means sweet gum tree.

Alba *(ahl bah')* Latin origin. The name means white, pure. Alba was the capital of the early Roman empire, as well as an ancient name of the Scottish Highlands. Variations: Alva.

Albina *(ahl bee' nah)* Latin origin. Derived from *alba*, the name means white. Diminutive: Alvinita. Variations: Albienta, Alveena.

Alegra *(ah lay' grah)* Latin origin. The name means joyous. The child bestowed with this name is honored with the enchanting designation of happiness or merriment. Variations: Elegria.

Alejandra *(ah lay hahn' dra)* Greek origin. Female version of Alejandro. The name combines the elements *alexein* (to defend or help) and *andros* (man): hence the name means defender of humankind. Baby girls who are named Alejandra are often named after the fifth-century saint St. Alejandro, known as the "sleepless one." He coordinated three hundred monks to sing night and day praising God ceaselessly in hope for the return of Christ. Diminutives: Asandra, Dina, Drina, Sandra, Zandra. Variations: Alehandra, Alejadra, Alejandria, Dejandra, Elejandra.

Aleta *(ah leh' tah)* Greek origin. Derived from the Greek name *alethea,* meaning truth.

Alicia *(ah lee' see ah)* Greek origin. In the Greek language the name means truth. Some believe the name is derived from the German *alexien* (to defend or come to one's aid): hence the name signifies helper or protector. Alyssa, a variation of this name, is currently one of the most popular names for girls in the United States. Diminutives: Chita, Licia. Variations: Alisha, Aliza, Alyssa.

Alma *(ahl mah)* Latin origin. Derived from the Spanish *alma* (soul). The current connotation of the name has come to mean the essence of life. Alternate translations signify the name to mean nurturing, loving, or kind. In the Hebrew language the name connotes girl or secret.

Almira *(ahl mee' rah)* Arabic origin. The name means princess.

Altagracia *(ahl' tah grah' tsee ah)* Latin origin. This name is a combination of the Spanish elements *alta* (tall, high, above) and *gracia* (grace, thanks, pardon). Hence the name connotes high grace. The name is given, especially in the Dominican Republic, in respect of the Virgin María, Our Lady of High Grace. Diminutives: Alta, Olta, Tatá. Variation: Altagratia.

Alvera *(ahl ber' ah)* German origin. The name means altogether cautious or extremely careful. In another sense, the name finds its roots in the Old English *æfhere.* This name combines the elements *æf* (elf) and *here* (army): hence the arrangement means elfin army. Variations: Alviria, Alvra.

Amada *(ah mah' dah)* Latin origin. Derived from the Latin *amada* (to love). Variation: Amadia.

Amalia *(ah mah lee' ah)* German origin. The name is derived from the German *amal* (work). Thus the name has come to signify the industrious or diligent one. Diminutives: Amalita, Lita, Maya, Melita. Variations: Amelia, Emala.

Amanda *(ah mahn' da)* Latin origin. The name means lovable, worthy of love, or deserving of love. There are many saints bearing this name. Diminutive: Mandy. Variation: Amata.

Amarilis *(ah mah ree' lees)* Greek origin. The name means sparkling stream. It is also the name of a plant that bears several white, purple, pink, or red lilylike flowers on a single stem. The shepherdess in pastoral poems by Virgil and Theocritus bore this beautiful name.

Amora *(ah mor' rah)* Latin origin. The name is derived from the Spanish *amor* (love).

Ana *(ah' nah)* Hebrew origin. The name means gracious or merciful. Greek form of Hannah. The original St. Ann is believed to have been Mary's mother and Jesus' grandmother. It is said that if Ana did not exist we would have to make her up—because grandmothers are that important to the Latino culture. Ana represents the vital link grandmothers play in sharing knowledge through the oral stories and legends, which connects the past with the present. She symbolizes our connection to our roots and the foundation for our pride in the people, *la raza*.

Anabel *(ah nah bell')* Hebrew origin. The name combines the elements Ana (graceful, gracious, merciful)

and Bella (beautiful): hence it means beautifully full
of grace and mercy. Variations: Anabelia, Anvela.

Analilia *(ah nah lee' lee ah)* Hebrew origin. The name
combines the elements of Ana (graceful, gracious, merciful) with Lilia, which is derived from the Latin *lilium*
(lily—the symbol of purity and innocence). The combination means graceful innocence.

Anarosa *(ah nah ro' sah)* Hebrew origin. The name
combines the elements of Ana (graceful, gracious, merciful) with Rosa (rose—the symbol of the Virgin
María). The combination means the merciful Virgin.

Anastasia *(ah nah stah' see ah)* Greek origin. Derived
from the Greek *anastasis,* meaning resurrection. Many
saints bore this name. Diminutives: Anasta, Nacha,
Stacy. Variations: Anastasa, Anastia.

Anatolia *(ah nah toe' lee ah)* Greek origin. The name
means one who comes from the east. Current translations have modified the name to symbolize daybreak,
sunrise, or dawn, even an awakening. Variations: An-
lalia, Antalina.

Andrea *(ahn dree' ah)* Greek origin. The name is a feminine version of Andrés (manly, strong): hence the
name means powerful, resilient woman, or womanly.
Andrés was one of Christ's first apostles. He was called
from his fishing nets by Jesus and asked to become a
fisher of men. He was martyred on an X-shaped cross.
Diminutive: Andreita. Variations: Andrianna, Andri-
ceta.

Angela *(ahn hel' lah)* Greek origin. The name is a feminine version of Angel (messenger or thoughts from
God). Angels are seen as spiritual beings who pass
messages to humans and are perceived as inspirations
of purity, goodness, and safety. Many call upon their
angels for guidance and protection. St. Angela Merici

founded the first teaching order for women. Diminutives: Angelina, Angelita.

Anica *(ah nee' cah)* Hebrew origin. Latin cognate of Hannah (God has shown favor).

Antonia *(ahn toe' nee ah)* Latin origin. The name means beyond price. In the Bible, Antonia was a fortress built by Herod. To name a child Antonia is often a form of honoring a favorite saint, St. Antonio of Padua. St. Antonio had an exceptional talent for preaching and teaching. Legend has it that the reason St. Antonio is known as the patron of lost property is because once when a novice took, without permission, St. Antonio's psalter he was ordered to return it by a terrifying apparition of the saint demanding the return of his property. To invoke this great martyr's help, you must have exhausted all your resources before you can say, "St. Antonio, St. Antonio, look around, look around. Something is lost and must be found." Diminutives: Tiffy, Tonia. Variations: Andona, Antoliana, Antoninetta.

Anunciación *(ah noon' see ah see own')* Spanish origin. The name means to announce and refers to Gabriel's announcement to Mary that she would give birth to the Christ child. A feast day of March 25 is dedicated to honor this event, known as the Annunciación. Diminutive: Inuncia. Variation: Annuciana.

Aparición *(ah pah ree see own')* Spanish origin. The name means the act of appearing and refers to Jesus Christ's appearance after his resurrection.

Apolonia *(ah po lo' nee ah)* Greek origin. The name means the light from the sun. Variations of this given name appear several times in the *Dictionary of Saints*. Yet the most revered of these saints was a poor woman who had her teeth pulled out by pincers and later became the patron saint of toothaches. Diminutives: Apolia, Palinaria, Poliana. Variations: Abulina, Apolinairia, Epolonia, Jolonia, Opalinaria.

Aponi *(ah poe' nee)* Native American origin. The name means butterfly. Butterfly represents change. It symbolizes mental clarity and is associated with air and wind.

Aquene *(ah key' nah)* Native American origin. The name means peace.

Aquilina *(ah kee lee' nah)* Latin origin. The name means like an eagle. This name appears several times in the *Dictionary of Saints*. Diminutive: Quina. Variation: Aquileya.

Arabella *(ah rah bay' lah)* Latin origin. The name means agreeing to a life of prayer. Another translation connotes beautiful altar. Variation: Arabelia.

Ariela *(ay ree aay' lah)* Hebrew origin. The name means lioness of God or hearth of God.

Arminda *(ahr meen' dah)* Hebrew origin. The name means safety and security offered by force. Variations: Armelinda, Armindina, Erminda.

Artemis *(are tay' mees)* Greek origin. The name means whole and perfect. She was the Greek goddess of the moon, hunting, and wild animals. There are many saints in the *Dictionary of Saints* with variations of this name. Diminutive: Micha. Variations: Artemisa, Hertenia.

Asela *(ah say ah)* Latin origin. Feminine version of Aselo. The name is believed to have derived from the Latin *asinus* (little donkey or burro). Another source states the name means slender ash tree. Diminutive: Aselina. Variation: Azela.

Aspasia *(ahs pah' see ah)* Greek origin. The name means welcome. This name is often applied to any exceedingly refined courtesan. It also appears twice in the *Dictionary of Saints*.

Asunción *(ah soon see own')* Latin origin. Derived from the Spanish *asunción* (assumption) and refers to the taking of the Virgin María's body from earth to heaven, known as the Assumption. Many saints of both genders were bestowed with this name. Diminutive: Chica. Variations: Ancencia, Ascensiana.

Athanasia *(ah tha nas' ee ah)* Greek origin. Feminine version of Athanasio. Derived from the Greek *athanasia* (immortality or without death, living eternally). A fourth-century scholar by this name is honored for his fight against Arian heresy. Diminutive: Atancia. Variations: Atanania, Atenacia.

Augustina *(ah goos tee' nah)*. Latin origin. Feminine version of Augustino, which is derived from *augustus* (revered, majestic, dignified, or exalted). Diminutives: Asta, Tina. Variations: Agostia, Agostina, Augustena, Austina.

Aurelia *(ow ray lee ah)* Latin origin. Derived from *aurum* (gold). It also has its roots from the old Roman family name of Aurēlius. Feminine form of Aurelio. A few saints bore this name.

Aurora *(ow roe' rah)* Latin origin. Derived from *aurum* (gold). It also has its roots from the old Roman family name of Aurēlius. The Roman goddess of dawn is believed to have taken this name because of the golden hues that fill the sky at daybreak.

Avanta *(ah bahn' tah)* Native American origin. The name means turtle. Turtle represents the womb of Mother Earth. It is the symbol for the power of feminine energy in all its forms: goddess, maiden, mother, or crone. It represents creativity, grounding, and patience. Variations: Awanta, Awanata.

Avellina *(ah bay yee' nah)* Spanish origin. Feminine version of Abellino. The name derives from hazel or from the city of Avellino, place of avellanos—hazelnut trees. Diminutive: Lina. Variations: Abelina, Avelinda.

Avendela *(ah bain day' lah)* Native American origin. The name means early day or daybreak. The name is usually bestowed upon a child born at dawn. Variation: Awendela.

Avenita *(ah bain ee' tah)* Native American origin. The name means fawn. According to Native American spirituality the deer represents gentleness, love, and compassion. It is through its gentle ways that the deer teaches us to find the heart and minds of those who would stand in our way. It is also said that deer can carry humans to the land of fairies if they so desire to meet these nature sprites. Variation: Awenita.

Azalia *(ah zah' lee ah)* Greek origin. The name means dry. It also can be a flower of vibrant red, purple, and pink petals that grows best in dry soil with little to no sunlight. Variation: Azalea.

Azucena *(ah zoo say' nah)* Arabic origin. Derived from the Spanish *azucena* (white lily). The lily is the symbol of purity and perfection. It is a common flower to give at the time of a death. In this way we honor the goodness of the deceased, and the pure light to where they have ascended.

Bárbara *(bar' bah rah)* Greek, meaning a foreigner. St. Barbara was believed to have been a young girl imprisoned in a tower by her father to keep men, especially Christian men, away. But as fate would have it, a doctor snuck into the room and succeeded in converting her. When her father ordered Barbara's head cut off he was struck by lightning.

Beatriz *(bay ah treex')* Latin origin. Derived from *beātus* (happy, blessed). The name has come to mean bringer of joy. Diminutives: Bebe, Beti, Tichi. Variations: Beatricia, Beatriz, Viatrice.

Belén *(bay lehn')* Hebrew origin. The name is derived from Bethlehem, the place of Christ's birth. The name means house of bread, possibly related to the taking of the host "the bread of Christ's body" during Mass; perhaps we can find a relation to this being the city where his body was housed. In addition, it could also be associated with the idea that through Jesus Christ's teachings and his actions Christians were given the substance, the core of their religion.

Belia *(bay lee' ah)* Spanish origin. Derived from the Spanish *bella*, the name means beautiful.

Beliarosa *(bay lee' ah ro' sah)* Spanish origin. The name combines the elements of *bella* (beautiful) with *rosa* (rose): hence the name means beautiful rose.

Belicia *(bay lee' see ah)* Latin origin. Derived from Elisabeth (God is my oath), this is also bestowed as a separate given name. Variations: Belica, Belita, Betina.

Belinda *(bay leen' dah)* German origin. The name means dragon. Alternate translations offer a combination of Belia and Linda: hence the name means beautiful. Still another meaning connotes shield of the bear.

Belloma *(bay low' mah)* Latin origin. The name means warlike or war goddess.

Bena *(bay' nah)* Native American origin. The name means pheasant. It can also be a diminutive for Benedicta.

Benedicta *(bay nay deek' tah)* Latin origin. The name means blessed. Female form of Benedicto. A girl is bestowed with this name usually in honor of St. Benedicto, father of the Holy Rule, also known as the Benedictine Rule. He was an impressive healer and a distinguished, respected teacher. Diminutive: Bena. Variation: Benita.

Bernadina *(bare nah dee' nah)* German origin. Female variant of Bernardo. The name combines the elements *bern* (bear) and *hard* (hearty, strong, powerful): hence the name means strong as a bear. Two illustrious saints bore this name: St. Bernardo of Montjoux, patron saint of skiers and mountaineers, and St. Bernardo of Clairvaux, patron saint of beekeepers, honey, and candle makers. Diminutive: Dina.

Bernicia *(bare nee' see ah)* Greek origin. The name means bringer of victory.

Betsabé *(bate sah bay')* Hebrew origin. Derived from the Hebrew Bathsheba, the name means daughter of oath or daughter of Sheba. In the Bible, the beautiful Batsheva was married to King David and bore his successor, King Solomon. Diminutive: Betsy. Variations: Batsheva, Besabela.

Bibiana *(bee bee ah' nah)* Latin origin. Derived from *vivere* (to live): hence the name means alive, living. It can also be translated to living a full life, aware of each moment. Cognates of this name appear five times in the *Dictionary of Saints*. Diminutive: Bibia. Variation: Bribiano.

Blanca *(blahn kah)* Spanish origin. The name literally means white. The name enjoyed much popularity throughout the world over the years, but has fallen down the charts for Hispanics as of late. Diminutives: Caca, Quita. Variations: Blanch, Vianca.

Bona *(bo' nah)* Latin origin. The name combines the elements of the Latin *bona* (good) with *dia* (divinity): hence the name means good goddess. She was the Roman goddess of fertility and women. She can be invoked for connecting with one's femininity. Variation: Bonita.

Brígida *(bree' hee dah)* Celtic origin. The name means strength or protecting. Although the name appears many times in the *Dictionary of Saints*, the most famous saint was the beloved Brigid of Ireland. Her patronage oversees wells, inspiration, fire, poetry, and healing. Her association with fire leads to the use of candles and rites of purification. Her celebration coincides with La Purificación de Nuestra Señora on February 2. Diminutive: Gidita. Variations: Brigda, Brigid, Briget.

Cabalina *(kah bah lee' nah)* Latin origin. Derived from Caballinus (belonging to a horse). Horses were brought to the Americas from Spain. Early explorers used them extensively. For a time the number and quality of horses you possessed determined your wealth. According to Native American tradition, horse medicine represents power.

Calida *(cah lee' dah)* Latin origin. The name means loving.

Caliopa *(kah lee' o pah)* Greek origin. The name is a combination of the Greek *kallos* (beautiful) and *ops* (voice): hence the name means beautiful voice. In Greek mythology, the Muse of epic poetry and expression bore this name. She was also the mother of Orpheus.

Calixto *(cah leeks' toe)* Greek origin. Derived from the Greek *kallos*, the name means the most beautiful. A cognate of this name, Calista, increased in popularity from near obscurity with the rise of a television star by that name. Variations of this name appear eight times in the *Dictionary of Saints*. Diminutive: Cali. Variations: Callista, Calistia.

Camelia *(kah may' lee ah)* Latin origin. Derived from the Latin *camilla* (virgin of unblemished character). A thirteenth-century martyr by this name chose to drown to preserve her virginity. A shrub with similar spelling produces waxy, roselike flowers. Variations: Camelea, Camellia.

Candelaria *(kan dah lah' ree ah)* Latin origin. This is the feminine form of Candelario. Derived from the Spanish *candelario* (wax candle). The name refers to the Catholic feast day known as La Purificatión de Nuestra Señora held on February 2. Many candles are lit as a symbol of illuminating the path in the middle of winter for the Holy Family on their visit to the temple. Diminutive: Candelina. Variation: Candelona.

Caparina *(kah pah ree' nah)* The name represents a type of butterfly.

Caridad *(kah ree dahd)* Latin origin. In Latin the name means dear, yet in Spanish it translates to charity. A young lady by this name, with her two sisters and mother, were martyred in the second century. The revered attributes of charity can be found in Corinthians 13. Slight alterations of this Bible verse are often cited in wedding ceremonies. Diminutives: Cari, Carucha.

Carina *(kah ree' nah)* Latin origin. The name means affectionate, loving. A saint who bore this name is honored on November 7. Variations: Cariana, Carima, Carimisa.

Carisa *(cah ree' sah)* Greek origin. The name means beautiful, graceful. An Italian cognate of this name translates to mean beloved or dear. In the fourth century a martyr by this name served and died with the order of St. Ursula, patron saint in charge of teaching young girls. They later were remembered as "the eleven who went up to heaven." Variation: Caríssima.

Carita *(cah ree' tah)* Latin origin. The name means charity.

Carlota *(kar lote' tah)* German origin. This is a popular feminine version of Carlos. The name comes from the German *karl* (strong or manly). Girls with this given name are often named after St. Carlos. St. Carlos spent his personal money and all his energy caring for the sick at the time of the plague. He also founded Sunday schools for the Confraternity of Christian Doctrine. Diminutive: Carly. Variations: Carlota, Carola.

Carmen *(kahr' mehn)* Hebrew origin. The name means vineyard, orchard, abundant meadow. Derived from Mount Carmel in Israel. This was a sacred place where early Christian monks gathered under the Order of Our Lady of Mount Carmel, a name bestowed in reverence of the Virgin María. Diminutive: Carmencita. Variation: Carmela.

Carolina *(kahr o lee' nah)* German origin. This is a feminine version of Carlos. The name comes from the German *karl* (strong or manly). Following the Hispanic tradition of giving a child a name that coincides with her surroundings, the name is quite popular for girls born in South or North Carolina.

Cassandra *(kah sahn' drah)* Greek origin. According to Greek mythology a woman by this name had the ability to foresee into the future.

Catarina *(cah tah ree' nah)* Greek origin. The name means pure or clean. Of all the Catarinas in the Roman martyrology the most famous are St. Catarina of Alejandría and St. Catarina of Siena. St. Catarina of Alejandría was a beautiful queen who won the admiration of the emperor. She did not return his affections, claiming she was already betrothed to Christ. This so infuriated the emperor that he ordered that she be executed on a spiked wheel. The torture machine did not kill her but in fact it wildly broke into pieces, killing many spectators. St. Catarina of Siena was important because she was not only a laywoman who was canonized, but she was also declared a Doctor of the Church even though she was illiterate. She received the stigmata and once had a vision of her marriage to Christ. She can be invoked as protection from fire because of an unforgettable miracle in which she was seen to have emerged from a fire wholly unscathed. Diminutives: Calina, Rina, Trina. Variations: Catalina, Cathalina.

Cecelia *(say see' lee ah)* Latin origin. Derived from the old Roman surname of Caecilius, which has its roots in *caecus* (blind, dim-sighted). St. Cecilia was forced to marry a pagan. During the wedding march she prayed to God through the music and is now known as the patron saint of musicians and poetry. She later converted her husband to Christianity. Diminutives: Cecy, Chela. Variations: Celicia, Celilia.

Celadonia *(say lah doe' nee ah)* The name refers to the swallow, a bird with dependable migratory patterns. The swallow's return to Mission San Juan Capistrano in southern California is so consistent that an annual celebration is planned every year to witness their magnificent return to their summer home. Diminutive: Cela. Variations: Aledonia, Celedoria.

Celestina *(say lay stee' nah)* Latin origin. Derived from the Roman family name of Caelius, which has its roots in *caelum* (heaven): hence the name has come to mean belonging to heaven. Diminutive: Celcia. Variation: Celstyna. `

Celina *(say lee' na)* Greek origin. The name refers to the splendor and light of the moon. It is also the namesake for the Greek goddess of the moon, known as Selene. Diminutives: Lina, Nina. Variations: Celene, Selena.

Chabela *(cha bay' lah)* Latin origin. This name also has its roots in Elisabeth (God is my oath). Yet it can be bestowed as a separate name. Diminutive: Chabi. Variation: Chavella.

Chalina *(cha lee' nah)* Latin origin. Derived from Rosa (rose).

Charo *(cha' roe)* Latin origin. The name has its roots in Rosa (rose). Variation: Chara.

Chenoa *(cheh no' ah)* Native American origin. The name means white dove. The dove is the bird of peace.

Chimalis *(chee mah' lees)* Native American origin. The name means bluebird.

Chitsa *(cheet' sah)* Native American origin. The name means fair one.

Cholena *(cho leh' nah)* Native American origin. The name means bird. Bird represents freedom. Freedom is found when living attuned to one's fundamental nature despite intolerance, fear, or prejudice. It symbolizes the essence of reflecting and sharing one's unique gift from God.

Cipriana *(see pree ah' nah)* Latin origin. This is a feminine version of Cipriano. The name means one who comes from Cyprus (a Mediterranean island off the coast of Turkey). Diminutive: Ciprianita.

Clara *(klah rah)* Latin origin. Derived from *clarus* (clear). The name also means bright. Although there were many saints who bore this name, St. Clara of Assisi is the most revered. In the thirteenth century she led her own order of "poor ladies" or "Poor Clares." Much loved by her nuns, St. Clara with her sisters lived a life of complete poverty, accepting only alms for their needs. She is known as a patron of television because of a vision she had of Jesus in the manger. Diminutive: Clarita. Variation: Clarisa.

Claudia *(klau' dee ah)* Latin origin. A female version of Claudio, the name is derived from the Roman surname of Claudius, which has its roots in *claudus* (lame). Variations of this name appear in the *Dictionary of Saints* over forty times. Diminutive: Clodita. Variation: Clodia.

Clemencia *(clay men' see ah)* Latin origin. Clemencia is the female version of Clemente. Usually baby girls baptized with this name are being named after St. Clemente, the fourth pope. The name means mild, tolerant, or merciful, and sometimes refers to the weather. Inhabitants living in towns named thus often enjoy pleasant and temperate weather. Diminutive: Lencha. Variation: Clemcia.

Clotilde *(cloe til' day)* German origin. The name means loud battle. King Clovis's wife was Clotilde; her life and child were saved in childbirth by St. Leonardo's fervent praying. Variations: Cleatilde, Clotilia.

Concepción *(cone sape see own')* Latin origin. The name means conception and refers to the sinlessness of the Virgin María at the moment of the Immaculate Conception. We pay tribute to this aspect of the Virgin on December 8. This name has waned in popularity. Diminutives: Choncha, Conchita. Variation: Conscenciana.

Conseja *(cone say' ha)* Latin origin. Derived from the Spanish *consejo* (counsel). The use of this name usually refers to the Virgin María and Nuestra Señora del Buen Consejo or Our Lady of Good Counsel. The feast day commemorating this event is April 26.

Constanza *(cone stahn' sah)* Latin origin. Derived from *constans* (constant, stable).

Consuela *(cone sway' lah)* Latin origin. The name means consolation or one who knows how to console, comfort, and soothe. Diminutives: Connie, Consolita. Variation: Consulla.

Coral *(co rawl')* Latin origin. This name is borrowed from the coral of the sea. The color of coral varies widely, including black, pink, red, white, and blue. Coral represents diplomacy and harmony. One of its most revered qualities is the quieting of emotions and the attainment of peace within the self.

Corazón *(kor ah zone')* Spanish origin. The name means heart. It refers to the Sacred Heart of Jesus.

Cordilia *(core dee' lee ah)* Latin origin. The name also means heart.

Corina *(co ree' nah)* Latin origin. The name means maiden. It is derived from Kore in Greek mythology, which is a cognate of Persephone, daughter of the goddess of spring and fertility. When Persephone ate pomegranate seeds from the underworld she was no longer a naïve maiden. She came to understand that the dark provides the contrast to joy so that we may realize our good fortune. She provides comfort in accepting the balance of comfort and discomfort, bad and good, joy and sorrow. According to legend, Persephone also acts as the bridge between the living and the dead. She reminds the living there is death so they will live a full life and she shows the dead the way to rebirth. Variation: Corinna.

Crescensia *(cray sen' see ah)* Latin origin. Derived from the Latin *crescentianus* (to grow). Possibly related to the crescent moon, which is waxing or growing into fullness. Diminutive: Checha. Variations: Cresanta, Cresentina.

Crispina *(crees peen' ah)* Latin origin. Female version of Crispin. Derived from *crispus* (curly). The name is traditionally bestowed in honor of St. Crispus of Tagora.

Cristina *(krees tee' nah)* Greek meaning Christian. St. Cristina the Astonishing is celebrated for her unique psychic abilities. She also possessed an unusually heightened sense of smell. She gave her life to prayer for the salvation of souls in purgatory after a near-death experience where she "awoke" at her own funeral. Diminutives: Chrystie, Nina, Tina. Variation: Crestena.

Cruza *(croo' zah)* Latin origin. Feminine version of Cruz. Derived from the Spanish *cruz* (cross or crucifix). Refers to the cross upon which Christ was killed. Diminutive: Crusita. Variation: Cruzelia.

Dahlia *(dah' lee ah)* Anglo-Saxon origin. This name is taken from a bright showy flower indigenous to Mexico and Central America. The flower was named after Dahl, an eighteenth-century Swedish botanist. Variations: Dalia, Dilana.

Damario *(dah mah' ree oh)* Latin origin. The name means calf. Variation: Damiris.

Damiana *(dah mee ah' nah)* Greek origin. Derived from the Greek *damān* (to tame) hence the name means tamer or guide. Feminine variation of Damian. Variation: Domiana.

Damita *(dah mee' tah)* Latin origin. The name means little noble lady.

Daniela *(dahn yell' ah)* Hebrew origin. The name means God judges or God is my judge. Feminine variation of Daniel.

Davida *(dah beed' ah)* Hebrew origin. Feminine variation of David. The name means beloved or friend. Twenty-six saints with this name are listed in the *Dictionary of Saints*.

Débora *(day' bo rah)* Hebrew origin. Derived from *devōrāh* (a bee), though the name has come to mean a swarm of bees. In another translation the name means to speak in kind words. In the Bible, Devorah was a prophetess who led a revolt against the Canaanites. Diminutive: Debby. Variations: Déborah, Devorah.

Decima *(day see' mah)* Latin origin. The name means tenth. Traditionally the name is only given to the tenth child.

Delfina *(dell fee' nah)* Latin origin. Derived from the Greek *delphin* (dolphin). The dolphin has long been a sacred animal to many indigenous peoples. Dolphins are regarded as highly intelligent, while still giving an example of the importance of play and laughter. The dolphin is symbolic of the breath of life, teaching us how to release emotions and find harmony. We see an example of this by her synchronized swimming, riding effortlessly with the rhythm of waves. The name is also related to the Latin Delphīna (woman from Delphi). Diminutive: Finita. Variations: Delphia, Dolphina.

Delicia *(day lee' see ah)* Latin origin. The name means that which causes pleasure, or delicious. Variations: Deliciano, Delia, Delyssa.

Demetria *(day may' tree ah)* Greek origin. The name means belonging to Demeter, the Greek goddess of agriculture and fertility. She oversees the development of all growing things, but in particular is the guardian of grain. When her daughter Persephone got lost in Hades' underworld Demeter anxiously grieved over her. It is said that Persephone ate six pomegranate seeds while in the underworld, and had to stay in that dark land for one month per seed. During her daughter's absence Demeter would not allow anything to grow; this marks our scarce seasons of fall and winter. The name appears fifty-three times in the *Dictionary of Saints*.

Desideria *(day see day' ree ah)* Latin origin. From the Latin word *desiderium* (desiring, yearning, or grief for an absent person). Other sources indicate this name originates from the French language and means to desire.

Destina *(day stee' nah)* Spanish origin. Derived from *destino* (destiny).

Deyanira *(day yah nee' rah)* Greek origin. The name means one who kills forcefully. In the Greek pantheon, the name was borne by Hercules's wife, who unwittingly caused his death in an attempt to win back his love. Variations: Dellanira, Deyamira.

Diana *(dee ah' nah)* Greek origin. Derived from the Latin Diviana, a name that means the divine one. In Roman mythology she is the goddess of the moon, hunting, forest animals, and woman in childbirth. In ancient Rome, Diana was praised for her athletic ability, strength, and grace. As a huntress her skills were unsurpassed.

Dina *(dee' nah)* Hebrew origin. Derived from *dīnāh* (judgment or judged). In the Bible, she was the daughter of Jacob. Variations: Dinah, Dinorha.

Dionisa *(dee o nee' sah)* Greek origin. The name means consecrated to Dionysius. Dionysius was the Greek god of fertility, wine, and revelry. Variations of this name appear sixty-eight times in the *Dictionary of Saints*. Diminutive: Nicha. Variations: Diocelina, Dionisea, Dioysia.

Dolores *(doe low' raze)* Latin origin. Derived from *dolores* (suffering or sorrows). The name refers to the seven sorrows the Virgin María suffered in her relationship with Jesus Christ. Diminutives: Dolorcitas, Dolorita, Lola, Lolita. Variations: Dolarez, Dolora.

Dorolinda *(doe roe lean' dah)* Latin origin. This name combines the elements of Dorotea (gift of God) and Linda (pretty or beautiful): hence the name means a beautiful gift from God.

Dorotea *(doe roe tay' ah)* Greek origin. The name is a combination of *dōron* (gift) with *theos* (God): hence the arrangement means a gift of God. Eighteen saints bore this name. Diminutives: Dori, Dorita, Lola. Variations: Dorinda, Dorotia.

Dulce *(dool' say)* Latin origin. Derived from *dulcis* (sweet or agreeable). Refers to "the sweet name of María," an attribute that is celebrated on September 12. Variation: Dulcinea.

Edelmira *(ā dell mee' rah)* German origin. Female version derived from the Germanic Adelmar, which combines the elements of *adal* (noble) with *mar* (race, people): hence the name means of noble race. Diminutives: Mima, Mimi. Variations: Almira, Edelmida.

Edenia *(ā day' nee ah)* Hebrew origin. This is a Spanish cognate of Eden, which has its roots in the Hebrew *ēdhen* (delight). In the Bible the Garden of Eden was the paradise where Adam and Eve first lived.

Edita *(ā dee' tah)* Anglo-Saxon origin. Derived from *ēad* (wealthy, rich, prosperous). Several saints bore this name. Variations: Edith.

Electa *(ā lake' tah)* Latin origin. The name means the selected one.

Electra *(ā lake' trah)* Greek origin. Derived from *ēlektōr* (shining). Another sense of the word translates the name to mean the millionth. Variation: Alectra.

Elena *(ā lay' nah)* Greek origin. A Spanish equivalent of the Greek Helen, which comes from Helenē, a name that has its roots in *ēlē* (light): hence the name has come to mean brilliant or resplendent. Another sense of the word translates the name to mean a woman of Greece. St. Elena is primarily remembered as the woman who found the cross on which Christ was crucified. Diminutive: Nena. Variations: Alena, Elaine, Helen.

Eleonor *(ā lay o nor')* Greek origin. A variant of Helenē, a name that has its roots in *ēlē* (light): hence the name has come to mean brilliant or shining one. In another source the name means "God of my youth." Diminutive: Nora. Variation: Eleonora.

Eleuthera *(ā lay yoo thay' rah)* Greek origin. Female form of Eleuterio. Derived from *eleutheria* (liberty, freedom). Over twenty saints appear with this name in the *Dictionary of Saints*. Diminutive: Tella. Variations: Eleutina, Elutena.

Elisabeth *(ā lee sah bet')* Hebrew origin. Derived from *elīsheba'* (God is my oath). Another source found this name to mean "God is fullness." According to the Bible, Elisabeth was the cousin of Mary and mother of St. John the Baptist. Diminutives: Betsi, Elsa, Nena. Variations: Elisabet, Elissa, Elizabé.

Eloisa *(ā low ee' sah)* German origin. The name means complete. Variations: Eloyza, Elysa.

Elsa *(el' sah)* German origin. Derived from Adelaida, a name that has its roots in *adal* (noble).

Elvira *(ell bee' rah)* German origin. The name means friendly, amiable. Diminutive: Vivita. Variation: Eviria.

Emalinda *(ā mah leen' dah)* Latin origin. Combination of Emma (grandmother; or in another sense it means strength) and Linda (pretty): hence the name means beauty in strength or the beauty that comes with age. In Latino culture, grandmothers are often the keepers of the family history and traditions, which they pass down through parables and stories. So culturally the name signifies an elderly wise woman or a magnificent sage.

Emelia *(ā may' lee ah)* German and Latin origin. It may be derived from the German *amal* (work): hence the name has come to mean industrious. Others believe the name has its roots in the Latin surname Aemilius, which comes from *aemulus* (to emulate or imitate in an effort to equal or excel). Diminutives: Emelina, Lila, Mila. Variations: Emila, Hemelia, Milana.

Emerenciana *(ā may ren see ah' nah)* Latin origin. Derived from the Latin Emerentius (worthy of merit), which has its roots in *ēmereo* (to earn, deserve, or warrant good things). Variations: Emenziana, Emeronsia.

Emma *(ā' mah)* Teutonic origin. The name means grandmother. In the younger German language the name is believed to have derived from *erm* (strength). Again this reiterates the strength found in a woman of age and substance.

Encarnación *(enn kar nah' see own')* Spanish origin. Derived from the Spanish *encarnación* (incarnation). Refers to the embodiment or manifestation of Christ, the second person of the Trinity, as the living form of God. The name symbolizes the holy word, the essence of God, becoming flesh.

Eneida *(ā nay dah)* Greek origin. Derived from *ainein* (to praise). Another source deems the name to mean to see. Variation: Enerida.

Engracia *(en grah' see ah)* Latin origin. Derived from *in gratia* (one who is in the Lord's grace or by the grace of God). Diminutive: Quique. Variation: Gracia.

Enriqua *(en ree' kah)* German origin. Female version of Enrique. The name is the Spanish equivalent of the German Heinrich (ruler of a residence or home ruler). Sixteen saints were bestowed with this name. Diminutives: Queta, Quetita. Variation: Enriqueta.

Epifania *(ā pee fah' nee ah)* Greek origin. Female version of Epifanio. Derived from *epiphaneia* (appearance, manifestation). The name relates to the Epiphany, which honors three events: the visit of the Three Wise Men, or Magi, the baptism of Jesus, and Jesus' first miracle at Cana. Diminutive: Pifania. Variations: Epephania, Esifania.

Eréndira *(ā rain' dee rah)* Aztec origin. The name means the one who smiles. According to Aztec legend she was the princess of Mexico. Variation: Alrendia.

Ernesta *(air nay' stah)* German origin. Feminine form of Ernesto. The name means earnest, steadfast, and sincere. Diminutive: Tina. Variation: Eristina.

Esmeralda *(ace may rall' dah)* Spanish origin. The name means emerald. This gem is known as the stone of successful love. It is said to instill domestic bliss and infuse loyalty and compassion within the self and others. Variations: Esmeranda, Ezmeralda.

Esperanza *(ace pay' rahn zah)* Spanish origin. The name means hope. Hope, faith, and charity/love are referred to in the Bible as the synonyms for God. Diminutive: Perita. Variations: Esperaza, Espranza.

Espiridiana *(ace pee ree' dee ah' nah)* Greek origin. Feminine form of Espiridión, which is an equivalent of the Greek Spiridion (basket maker), a name that has its roots in *spīra* (coil, wreath, spiral). Three saints have borne this name. Diminutive: Spriana. Variations: Espedia, Espiridiosa.

Estebana *(ā stay bah' nah)* Greek origin. Female form of Esteban. Derived from the Latin Stephanus, which has its roots in the Greek *stephanos* (a crown, or wreath that adorns the head). Although there are eighty-two saints bestowed with this name, the one most honored was St. Esteban, the first Christian martyr, a powerful preacher and one of the seven deacons who assisted the apostles. Diminutive: Stefa. Variations: Estafina, Estevava.

Estela *(ace tay' lah)* Latin origin. The name means star, a celestial constellation. Diminutives: Nita, Telita. Variations: Estilla, Estrell.

Ester *(ace tare')* Persian origin. The name also means star, a heavenly body. Diminutive: Esterlita. Variations: Estar, Esteranza.

Estsanatlehi *(est san at' lu hee)* Navajo origin. The name means woman who changes. Estsanatlehi is known as the goddess of creation. She symbolizes the ever-changing earth, which is constantly renewing itself with plants growing, dying, and being born again each year. The origin of her name comes from her own changing form: in the spring she appears as a maiden, during the late summer and fall she is the mother, and during the winter she is depicted as an old woman. She is also the creator of all songs and rituals associated with the Blessingway, ceremonies performed to create hope and good fortune.

Etenia *(eh teh' nah)* Native American origin. The name means wealthy.

Eufemia *(ā oo fay' mee ah)* Greek origin. The name combines the elements *eu* (good, fine) and *phēmē* (voice): hence the name means having a fine voice. Another source translates the name to mean of good report. Sixteen saints bore this name. Diminutive: Femia. Variations: Eufenia, Euphemius.

Eufrasia *(ay ooh frah' see ah)* Greek origin. The name means full of joy. Of the fifteen saints bestowed with this name the most remarkable was a young girl of Constantinople who at age seven became a nun. Diminutive: Fresia. Variations: Eufacia, Eufraria.

Eugenia *(ā oo hay' nee ah)* Greek origin. Female form of Eugenio. Derived from *eugenēs* (well-born, aristocratic). The name appears fifty-four times in the *Dictionary of Saints.* Diminutive: Queña. Variation: Egenia.

Eulalia *(ā oo lah' lee ah)* Greek origin. The name combines the elements of *eu* (well, good) and *lalein* (to talk): hence the name means she who speaks well. Diminutives: Lali, Layita. Variations: Eralia, Eulilia.

Eunice *(ā oo nee' say)* Greek origin. The name combines the elements of *eu* (good, fine, happy) with *nikē* (victory): hence the name means fine or happy victory. Three saints bore this name. Variation: Eunecia.

Eutimia *(ā oo tee' mee ah)* Greek origin. The name means one who is greatly honored. The name appears nineteen times in the *Dictionary of Saints.*

Eutropia *(ā oo tro' pee ah)* Greek origin. The name combines the elements *eu* (good, happy) and *tropis* (sediment of wine): hence the name has come to mean of good spirit.

Eva *(ā bah)* Hebrew origin. Derived from *hawwāh* (life). From the Bible, we know Eva as the first woman and mother of all human life. Diminutive: Evita. Variation: Ava.

Evangelina *(ā bahn hay lee' nah)* Latin origin. Derived from *evangelium* (evangelist, bearer of good news). The name refers to the four evangelists of Christianity: Matthew, Mark, Luke, and John. Los Lobos, one of the first Hispanic bands to be widely accepted in both Hispanic and Anglo cultures, sings a song entitled *Evangeline,* which increased the name's popularity for a short time. Variations: Evangela, Evangeline.

Exaltación *(ayks ahl tah see own')* Latin origin. The name means to glorify or praise. The name refers to the feast on September 14, known as the Exaltación de la Santa Cruz, an event that honors and commemorates the miraculous removal of the holy cross from Jerusalem. Diminutive: Salto. Variation: Asoltación.

Fabiola *(fah bee o' lah)* Latin origin. Derived from the Roman surname Fabius, which has its roots in *faba* (a bean). Variation: Fabola.

Fatima *(fah' tee mah)* Arabic origin. The name is bestowed in honor of Our Lady of Fatima, who in 1917 appeared to three shepherd children, Lucia, Jacinta, and Francisco, from the village of Fatima, Portugal. She requested that every person be devoted to the immaculate heart of the Virgin María. To prove her authenticity she predicted a miracle in the sky, in which the sun twirled in the sky, threw off a rainbow of colors, then plummeted to the earth.

Faustina *(fows tee' nah)* Latin origin. Female version of Faustino. Derived from Faustus (bringer of good luck), which has its roots in *fauste* (prosperous, lucky, fortunate). The name appears eighty-seven times in the *Dictionary of Saints*. One of two twentieth-century saints, St. Faustina was blessed with a vision of Jesus Christ every day of her life. Diminutive: Fata. Variation: Faustia.

Febe *(fay' bee)* Greek origin. Derived from the Greek Phoebe, which has its roots in *phoibos* (bright or shining). It refers to the luminosity of the moon.

Felipa *(fay lee' pah)* Greek origin. Feminine form of Felipo. Combines the elements of *philos* (loving) with *hippos* (horses): hence the name means lover of horses. Baby girls given this name are usually named after Philip the Apostle. Diminutive: Felepita. Variations: Felopa, Phillipa.

Felixa *(fay leek' sah)* Latin origin. The name means fortunate or happy. Felixa is the female version of Felix.
St. Felix escaped persecution with the help of an angel.
He hid in a cave, whereupon a spider immediately spun
an elaborate web that covered the entrance of the cave,
concealing the hidden man. He was known for his
compassion and generosity. Variations: Felecita, Felic-
ity, Felixta.

Fidela *(fee day' lah)* Latin origin. Derived from *fidelis*
(faithful, loyal, trustworthy). In the Victorian period
wedding portraits were drawn with dogs in the picture
because they represented loyalty: hence the pet name
Fido for dogs became popular. Diminutive: Lela. Variation: Filelia.

Filomena *(fee low may' nah)* Greek origin. Combination of the elements *philos* (loving) and *menos* (spirit):
hence the name means loving spirit. Also means
daughter of light. The name was borne by a thirteen-
year-old virgin martyr of early Rome who refused the
affections of her ruler. Her personal belongings, in addition to a phial of blood, the recognized sign of martyrdom, were found in 1802. Diminutive: Mena.
Variation: Philomena.

Flavia *(flah' bee ah)* Latin origin. The name means yellow. This name is traditionally bestowed upon a child
with blond hair.

Florencia *(flo ren' see ah)* Latin origin. Derived from
florens (blooming, abundant, burgeoning). The name
appears sixty-six times in the *Dictionary of Saints*. Diminutive: Florita. Variations: Flora, Florida, Florinda.

Francisca *(frahn sees' kah)* Latin origin. Derived from
the French *franc* (free). The name also means from
France or a freeman. Francisca is the female version
of Francisco, therefore girls with this name are often
named after St. Francis de Asís, a man of exceptional

spiritual insight, living the gospel as it was actually written—an outstanding feat for his times. It is said a young priest in his order was very excited to accompany St. Francis in his sermon to the people. Finally the saint and apprentice went to the open market together. After spending two hours speaking with the people about their day, their lives, their relationships they headed for home. Exasperated, the young priest asked when they were going to give their sermon. The patient saint replied that they already had—that they'd taught and preached by being an example of faith, goodheartedness, and kindness. Diminutive: Chica. Variation: Frencisia.

Fuensanta *(fwehn sahn' tah)* Latin origin. Derived from the elements *fons* (fount, source) and *sanctus* (holy, sacred): hence the name means sacred fount or holy source. Refers to another idealized aspect of the Virgin María: Nuestra Señora de la Fuensanta, Our Lady of the Holy Fount. Diminutive: Fuenta.

Gabriela *(gah bree ay lah)* Hebrew origin. Derived from *gavhrī' ēl* (God is strong or God is my strength). Gabriela is the female variation of Gabriel. In addition to being the messenger of God, it is believed on the last day on earth Gabriel will blow his trumpet, calling humans home to heaven. Variations of this name are found twenty-four times in the *Dictionary of Saints*. Diminutives: Bel, Gabi. Variations: Gabrieala, Graviella.

Genaida *(hay nigh' dah)* Greek origin. Derived from *genēs* (born). Other sources say the name means of noble birth.

Generosa *(hay nay ro' sah)* Spanish origin. The name means generous.

Genoveva *(hay no bay' bah)* Celtic and Greek origin. Composed of the elements *genos* (people, clan) and *eva* (life or the first woman): hence the name means "the soul or essence of our clan." In another translation the name means white or the white foam of a wave. Traditionally one of the most popular names, it boasts over one hundred variations. Variations: Genevive, Jeneva.

Gertrudis *(hare troo' dees)* German origin. Derived from the elements *ger* (spear) and *trut* (dear): hence the name means one who cherishes the spear. Diminutive: Trudel. Variation: Gertrudia.

Gisela *(hee say' lah)* German origin. The name means pledge or promise.

Glenda *(glen dah')* Anglo-Saxon origin. The name means wholesome, fair, and good.

Gloria *(glow' ree ah)* Latin origin. The name means fame, glory, and grandeur. Refers to the magnificence of heaven. Diminutives: Glori, Glorinda.

Godeliva *(go day lee' bah)* German origin. An equivalent of Godiva (God's gift).

Graciela *(grah see ay' lah)* Latin origin. Derived from *gratia* (gracious, amiable). The name relates to the grace of God, blessing, and gift of life. Variations of this name appear sixteen times in the *Dictionary of Saints*. Diminutives: Chelita, Cheya. Variations: Graciana, Gracila, Graziella.

Griselda *(gree sale dah)* German origin. Derived from *gries* (gray, stone). This name was bestowed upon a medieval woman whose husband continually subjected her to tests of loyalty and fidelity.

Guadalupe *(gwah dah loo' pay)* Spanish origin. The name means valley of the wolves. Our Lady of Guadalupe is of paramount importance and reverence in the Latino culture. In 1531, she appeared to a humble Mexican on his way to receive Christian instruction.

She was covered in a turquoise cloak, the same color associated with the Aztec mother goddess Tonantzin, and had dark skin and hair. In the native tongue, she asked that a temple dedicated to her be built on Tepeyac Hill, where she could love and protect the people. The frightened man timidly appeared before the bishop begging for the Virgin's request. The clergyman demanded proof. Dejected, the poor convert returned to the Virgin of Guadalupe. With tears in his eyes he related his visit with the bishop. She offered him Castillian roses, a spectacular sight considering they were out of season, as proof of her authenticity. "For," she added, "I am the Mother of all of you who live on this land." The Indian returned with the roses in his cloak, or tilma. When he opened his tilma for the bishop an image of the Virgin of Guadalupe appeared upon it. With her head slightly tilted, she shone radiant as the sun with jewels sparkling at her feet and the Christ child bearing her. The news of the miracle spread quickly. The church was built and thousands were converted. The Virgin of Guadalupe represents the acceptance of the Indian people, by incorporating the European and indigenous spirituality. Since her first apparition, the Lady has protected the Mexican people against floods, earthquakes, and epidemics. She is responsible for many miracles and is loved beyond measure. Her fiesta, a pilgrimage into the heart of Mexico for thousands of Catholics, is held on December 12. Diminutives: Guada, Lupe, Lupita. Variations: Guadalupa, Guadelupi.

Guillermina (*ghee yare mee' nah*) German origin. Female version of Guillermo. Compounding of the elements *willeo* (will, resolution) and *helm* (helmet, protection): hence the name means helmet of protection or defender with a strong determination. Diminutives: Minita, Vilma. Variations: Gellermina, Guerma.

Hermelinda *(air may leen' dah)* German origin. The name means shield of power. Diminutive: Mela. Variations: Ermelinda, Hermelina.

Herminia *(air mee' nee ah)* German origin. Female version of Herminio. The name is an arrangement of *heri* (army) and *man* (man): hence the name means warrior or soldier. From another source the name means sacred place.

Hernanda *(air nahn' dah)* German origin. The name means to make peace.

Honoria *(o no' ree ah)* Latin origin. Derived from the Latin *honor* (esteemed, respected, revered). The name appears fifty-one times in the *Dictionary of Saints*. Variation: Hanora.

Hortencia *(or tane' see ah)* Latin origin. Derived from the Roman surname of Hortensius (gardener), which has its roots in *hortus* (garden). Diminutive: Chencha. Variations: Hortecia, Hortnecia.

Ida *(ee' dah)* German origin. Derived from *īd* (diligent, labor): hence the name has come to mean a diligent worker.

Idalia *(ee dah' lee ah)* Greek origin. The name means "I see the sun." The name is borrowed from an ancient site dedicated to Aphrodite, the goddess of love. Variation: Idalea.

Idolina *(ee doe lee nah)* Latin origin. Derived from *idolum* (image, likeness). Variation: Indolina.

Idonia *(ee doe nee' ah)* Latin origin. Derived from the Latin surname of Idonesu (of good disposition).

Ifigenia *(ee fay hay' nee ah)* Greek origin. Derived from Iphigeneia (of royal birth). Diminutive: Effa. Variations: Efigencia, Efigenia.

Iluminada *(ee loo' mee nah' dah)* Latin origin. The name means illuminated.

Imelda *(ee mell' dah)* German origin. An arrangement of the elements *irmen* (entire, complete) and *hild* (battle): hence the name means the entire battle. Variations: Amelda, Imelde.

Immaculada *(ee ma cyoo lah' dah)* Latin origin. The name is bestowed in honor of the Immaculate Conception, which falls on December 8.

Indiana *(een dee ah' nah)* Latin origin. Derived from Indianus (of the East Indies), which has its roots in *india* (hind).

Inés *(ee nays')* Greek origin. Derived from *hagnos* (pure, chaste, holy). The name is a Spanish cognate of Agnes. St. Inés was dedicated to Christ because of her conviction to remain a virgin. When she was only thirteen years old, she refused to marry a Roman governor's son who had fallen in love with her. When he threatened to take her by force, he was immediately struck blind and then miraculously cured by the chaste Inés herself. Diminutives: Agnesita, Inésita. Variations: Agnese, Inez, Ynez.

Inocencia *(een oh sehn see ah)* Latin origin. The name means innocence. The name is often bestowed in reference to the innocence of the Virgin María. Variation: Inocenta.

Irene *(ee ray' nay)* Greek origin. Derived from *eirēnē* (peace): the name has come to mean lover of peace. The name appears twenty-one times in the *Dictionary of Saints*. Diminutives: Nea, Renequita. Variations: Ireña, Yrinea.

Iris *(ee' rees)* Greek origin. The name means rainbow. Iris was known as the goddess of the rainbow.

Irma *(eer' mah)* German origin. The name means force. Variations: Ermma, Irmalenda.

Isabela *(ee sah bell' ah)* Hebrew origin. Equivalent to Elizabeth, which has its roots in *elīshabà* (God is my oath or affirmation). Two queens of Spain bore this name in addition to four saints. Diminutives: Belita, Chela, Isa. Variations: Isabelle, Sabela.

Isidora *(ee see doe' rah)* Greek origin. Derived from the elements Isis (Egyptian goddess; see Isis, next entry) and *dōron* (gift): hence the name means gift of Isis. The name appears thirty-one times in the *Dictionary of Saints*. Diminutives: Dorina, Ysa. Variations: Isedora, Ysidora, Ysidra.

Isis *(ee' sees)* Egyptian origin. The name means both earth and throne. Isis was an Egyptian goddess who ruled everything that had to do with moisture, wetness, daytime—especially the dawn, fertility, and love. Her husband, Osiris, was slain by his jealous brother, yet through her unyielding love Isis brought her beloved back to life long enough to conceive a child. The birth of her son, Horus, coincides with Christmas and the winter solstice. This myth represents the changing of the seasons, with Osiris being the essence of nature that dies and is reborn, and Isis the power of love, which can create new life out of the deceased. She was revered as the Great Mother Goddess of the Universe. Isis is traditionally pictured with a headdress of a sundisk placed between two cow horns.

Jacaranda *(hah cah rahn' dah)* Tupi-Guarani (Brazilian) origin. The name means strong odor. This flower's foliage is divided and adorned with large lavender flower clusters.

Jacinda *(hah seen' dah)* Latin origin. Borrows the name from the hyacinth flower. According to Greek mythology a beautiful youth by this name was adored and accidentally killed by Apollo. Variation: Jacinta, Jacynthe.

Jada *(hah' dah)* Anglo-Saxon origin. Borrows this name from the precious gem. Jade was important to the Mayan culture. The stone was revered as the "sovereign of harmony." It was believed to facilitate peace, harmony, and resourcefulness. It is also known as the dream stone and the stone of fidelity. Placed under one's pillow at night, jade is used to help one remember and assess dreams. Variation: Jaida.

Jazmín *(hahs meen')* Arabic origin. Derived from *yāsmīn* (jasmine), which is the name of a subtropical plant. The flowers are strongly fragrant and come in yellow, red, and white. Often the flower is used in perfume or for scenting teas.

Jemsa *(hem' sah)* Spanish origin. The name means gem or precious stone.

Jesusa *(hay soo' sah)* Hebrew origin. The name is the female form of Jesus, which derives from *yehōshū'a* (the Lord saves, God is my salvation). Other sources indicate this name is the shortened form of María de Jesus.

Jimena *(hee meh' nah)* Hebrew origin. The name means she who has been heard.

Joaquina *(hwah kee' nah)* Hebrew origin. Female version of Joaquin. The name means God will establish. Variation: Joaquine.

Josefa *(hoe say' fa)* Hebrew origin. A female version of José. Derived from *yōsēf* (may God increase or God will add). Baby girls named Josefa derive their name from St. José, the carpenter and the earthly father of Jesus. José took great care of the holy family. He is remembered as a just man, exhibiting the human qualities of being upright, meritorious, and true. It is said he was left with his dreams and the work of his hands. He can be invoked for the healing power of letting go and letting God. His obedience and dedication to God's will is highly regarded. Variations: Josée, Josepha.

Joyita *(hoy ee' tah)* Latin origin. The name means little jewel.

Juana *(hwahn' ah)* Hebrew origin. Juana is the popular female version of Juan. The name means God is gracious. Juan the baptist, a cousin of Jesus, is remembered as the greatest of all prophets. Diminutive: Juanita.

Judit *(hoo' deet)* Hebrew origin. The name means praised.

Julia *(hoo lee ah)* Latin origin. The name means downy-bearded or youthful. Feminine version of Julio. Diminutive: Juli. Variations: Juliena, Julieta.

Larrina *(lah ree' na)* Latin origin. Derived from *laurus* (laurel). Variation: Larina.

Laura *(lah oo' rah)* Latin origin. The name is also derived from *laurus* (a bay or laurel tree). A ninth-century nun and saint of Cordova bestowed with this name was martyred in boiling pitch. Diminutive: Larissa. Variation: Laurela.

Laurentia *(lah rehn chee ah)* Latin origin. Derived from Laurentius (a man from Laurentum), a town that derived its name from *laurus* (a bay or laurel tree). St. Lorenzo was a third-century martyr, one of the seven deacons of Rome, and is believed to rescue a soul from purgatory every Friday. When he was commanded to hand over all the wealth of the church he presented to the authorities hundreds of poor and handicapped people, widows, and orphans, proclaiming, "Here is the church's wealth." He was arrested and tortured but is said to have never lost his serenity and humor throughout the horrible agonies to which he was subjected.

Lavinia *(lah bee' nee ah)* Latin origin. A feminine form of Latinus (from Latium, the area surrounding and including ancient Rome). According to Roman mythology she was the daughter of King Latinus. She later became the wife of Aeneas and was regarded as the mother of the Roman people.

Leah *(lay' ah)* Hebrew origin. Derived from *lā'āh* (to tire or exhaust). According to the Bible she was Jacob's first wife.

Leda *(lay' dah)* Greek origin. According to Greek mythology, she was the mother of Clytemnestra, Helenē of Troy, and Pollux and Castor. Variations: Laida, Leida.

Leila *(lay ee' lah)* Arabic origin. The name means dark beauty, beauty of the night. Variation: Leilani.

Leocadia *(lee o kay dee ah)* Greek origin. Derived from *ēlē* (light, brilliant). The name means glorious brilliance. The name was borne by a second-century virgin martyr from Spain who rose from her tomb to defend the virginity of the Virgin María. Variation: Leocadra.

Leonarda *(lay o nar' dah)* German origin. Composed of the elements of *lewo* (lion) and *hart* (bold, strong, brave): hence the name means strong as a lion or lion bold. There were ten saints who bore this name.

Leoncia *(lay own' see ah)* Latin origin. Female version of Leoncio. Derived from *leo* (lion). Diminutive: Liancia.

Leonor *(lay o nor')* Greek and German origin. This name boasts a few translations. The first is that it is a cognate of Eleanor, which is a variant form of the Greek Helenē (light, illumination). Others believe the

name derives from the German Lewenhart, which is
the source for the male Leonard, a name that has its
roots in the elements *lewo* (lion) and *hart* (bold, strong,
brave): hence the name means strong as a lion. Still
other sources state the name means compassionate or
kindhearted.

Leticia *(lay tee' see ah)* Latin origin. Derived from *lae-
titia* (delight, happiness): hence the name has come to
mean she who brings happiness or is delightful. Diminutives: Leti, Ticha. Variation: Leatrice.

Liberada *(lee bay rah' dah)* Latin origin. Derived from
Liberatus (she who has been liberated or freed), which
has its roots in *liberatus* (to liberate, set free). The
name was borne by a mystical saint of Portugal who
grew a beard in order to maintain her virginity. Diminutive: Libra. Variation: Liberda.

Libia *(lee' bee ah)* Latin origin. The name means from
Libya, a country in northern Africa. Variation: Livia.

Lilia *(lee' lee ah)* Latin origin. Derived from *lilium*
(lily). The lily is regarded as the flower of hope, purity,
new beginnings, and innocence. The flower is also a
symbol of spring. The flower is sacred to the Virgin
María. Variations: Lili, Liliana.

Linda *(leen' dah)* Spanish origin. The name means
pretty or beautiful.

Lissilma *(lee seel' mah)* Native American origin. The
name means to be there, to be available for someone.

Lorena *(low ray' nah)* French origin. The name means
from the territory of Lothair.

Lourdes *(lure' days)* Basque origin. The name means
craggy slope. Also borrowed from a town in south-
western France where St. Bernadette received visions
of the Virgin María in 1858.

Lucía *(loo see' ah)* Latin origin. Derived from *lux* (light). The light represents the coming of the dawn and beginning of new thought. To ancient people, it symbolized the awareness that with the rise of the sun everything will once again be all right. Some believe this perhaps is the reason St. Lucia's feast day falls near the winter solstice and return of the sun and warmth. Diminutive: Lucecita. Variations: Lucila, Lucilda.

Lucinda *(loo seen' dah)* Latin origin. Derived from *lux* (light). This is a variant form of Lucía also bestowed as a given name in honor of St. Lucía. Legend has it that St. Lucía presented her eyes on a platter to the man who, enraged by her lack of love for him, condemned and admonished her as a Christian.

Lucrecia *(loo kreh' syah)* Latin origin. Derived from *lux* (light). The name means she who brings light.

Luisa *(loo ee' sah)* German origin. Composition of the elements *hloud* (famous, glorious) and *wīg* (war, battle): hence the name means glorious battle or famous in war. St. Luisa founded the Daughters of Charity. She and her sisters worked with the poorest of Paris and is believed to have inspired Florence Nightingale to develop a strong sense of administering care to the sick some three hundred years later. Diminutives: Isa, Lulu. Variation: Luisiana.

Luminosa *(loo mee no' sah)* Latin origin. The name means luminous, radiant.

Luz *(loose)* Latin origin. Derived from *lux* (light). The name is given in honor of Nuestra Señora de la Luz, Our Lady of Light. Diminutives: Lucina, Lula. Variations: Lusa.

Macaria *(mah kah' ree ah)* Greek origin. Female version of Macario. Derived from *makaros* (blessed or fortunate one). Variation: Macarria.

Magdalena *(mahg dah lane' ah)* Hebrew origin. The name means of or from Magdala, a town on the shore of Galilee. The inspiration for this popular name usually comes from Mary Magdalena. She is often said to have been the first apostle because the risen Christ first appeared to her and the news of the resurrection was first entrusted to her. She also waited at the foot of the cross at the time of the crucifixion. Diminutive: Malena. Variation: Magdalén.

Manuela *(mahn well' lah)* Hebrew origin. Female variant of the male Manuel. Derived from the Greek Emmanouēl, a name that has its roots in the Hebrew *'immānūēl* (God is with us). According to the Bible this name means a descendant of David, therefore it signifies the Messiah.

Maravilla *(mah rah bee' yah)* Latin origin. Derived from *mīrābilis* (marvelous, magnificent, breathtaking). Variation: Marivel.

Marcelina *(mar say lee' nah)* Latin origin. Still another name bestowed as a stand-alone given name that is derived from Marcos (descendant from Mars, the war god). Variation: Marsalina.

Marcia *(mar' see ah)* Latin origin. Marcia is a female version of Marcos. Derived from Marcus (of Mars or warlike). Mars was the Roman god of war. Another source states the name means hammer. Still others believe it derives from *mas* (manly) or the Greek *malakoz* (gentle, tender). A child is usually bestowed with this name in devotion to Marcos, one of the apostles.

Marciana *(mar see ah' nah)* Latin origin. Derived from Marcus, the name means one belonging to Mars.

Margarita *(mar gah ree' ta)* Greek origin. Derived from *margaron* (pearl). St. Margarita was a seventeenth-century nun. She is usually depicted with a heart in flames because she had visions of Jesus showing her a similar heart, which has come to be known as the Sacred Heart. Diminutives: Margó, Rita. Variations: Margarit, Marguerita.

María *(mah ree' ah)* Egyptian origin. The name means beloved. From the Hebrew language the name means sea of sorrow or bitterness. Still other definitions offer rebellion, lady, or wished-for child as alternate meanings. Yet since the Mother of Christ is the most revered and sacred of all saints it makes sense that her name most importantly means beloved lady. Her most celebrated attribute was her obedience to God and acceptance of His will. Her declaration "let it be with me according to your word" is the foundation and inspiration for many spiritual people. It is believed that without the goodness of God's divine plan, His omnipotence, harmony, and right order this world would know only utter chaos. Possibly this is why her pledge to God is often perceived as the turning point for the salvation of humankind. Since María is a highly popular name other names are often added to it to distinguish María's fine attributes. Variation: Mariquita.

María Amelia *(mah ree' ah ah may' lee ah)* Combination of María (beloved lady) and Amalia (work): hence the name means the work of our beloved Lady.

María Antonieta *(mah ree' ah ahn twah nay' tah)* Combination of María (beloved lady) and Antoinetta (beyond price): hence the name means our beloved Lady is priceless.

Maríadela *(mah ree' ah day' lah)* Combination of María (beloved lady) and Adela (noble): hence the name means the dignity of our beloved Lady.

Mariaelena *(mah ree' ah lay nah)* Combination of María (beloved lady) and Elena (light): hence the name means the light found in our beloved Lady.

María Josefa *(mah ree' ah yo sef' ah)* Quite popular combination of María (beloved lady) and Josefa (God will increase): hence the name means with faith in our beloved Lady, God will add goodness to your life.

Mariana *(mah ree ah' nah)* Combination of María (beloved lady) and Ana (merciful): hence the name means our merciful Lady.

Maribel *(mah ree bell')* Combination of María (beloved lady) and Belle (beautiful): hence the name means our beautiful Lady.

Marina *(mar ree' nah)* Latin origin. Feminine form of Marino. Derived from *marinus* (mariner, man of the sea).

Mariposa *(mah ree poe' sah)* Latin origin. The name means butterfly. According to Native American spirituality, due to the many changes in its form the butterfly represents transformation, especially that connected to the growth of character. The four stages it moves through are connected to the following cycles: the egg stage equates to the beginning of all things; the larval stage corresponds to the point at which one makes a decision to change; the cocoon stage represents developing a project, aspect of oneself, or idea; and leaving the chrysalis is akin to sharing the rewards and splendor of hard work with humankind.

Marisa *(mar ree' sah)* Combination of María (beloved lady) and Luisa (famous in battle): hence the name means our beloved Lady victorious in the battle for good.

Marisol *(mah ree sole')* Combination of María (beloved lady) and Soledad (solitude): hence the name means our Lady of Solitude.

Maristela *(mah ree stay' lah)* Combination of María (beloved lady) and Estella (star): hence the name means our heavenly Lady.

Marta *(mar' tah)* Hebrew origin. The name means lady of the house. Those enduring the drudgery of housework can find strength in St. Marta. This saint worked tirelessly serving other people for the sake of Christ, even though she felt bored and uninspired by this unappreciated housekeeping. Her endurance and fortitude were rewarded when Christ took the treacherous journey through Bethany and raised her brother Lazarus from the dead. Diminutive: Martina.

Matilde *(mah teel' day)* German origin. The name combines the elements *maht* (might or power) and *hild* (battle): hence the name means powerful in battle and even battle maid. There were four saints bestowed with this name. Diminutive: Tilda. Variation: Mathilde.

Maxima *(mahks' ee mah)* Latin origin. Female form of Maximo. Derived from Maximus, a name that translates literally to mean the greatest.

Maximila *(mahks' ee mee' lah)* Latin origin. Female form of Maximiliano. Combination of two Latin names: Maximus (the greatest) and Aemmiliānus, a name that has its roots in *aemulus* (emulating, trying to be like another). Seven saints bore this name.

Maya *(my' yah)* Greek origin. The name means mother. Derived from Maia, the Greek goddess of spring and rebirth; hence today people revere her as a representation of Mother Earth. Maya is not only the patron of the earth and all its inhabitants; she is the embodiment of the earth itself. She is known as the force that creates new life. She is the namesake for the month of May. Many people across the globe celebrate her on the first of May, known as May Day. According to mythology she is the youngest of seven daughters of

Atlas who became the seven stars of the Pleiades when he was made to hold the world on his shoulders.

Melisa *(may lee' sah)* Greek origin. The name directly translates to mean a bee.

Mercedes *(mare say' days)* Latin origin. Derived from *merced* (mercy, compassion). The name is bestowed to honor the unconditional compassion and mercy of the Virgin María. The feast day for Nuestra Señora de las Mercedes, Our Lady of Mercy, is held on September 24.

Mersera *(mare say' rah)* This name combines the names Mercedes (mercy) and Sara (princess): hence the name means merciful princess.

Miguela *(mee gell' lah)* Hebrew origin. Female form of Miguel. Derived from *mīkhā'ēl* (who is like God). Miguel the Archangel is the leader of the army of good who battle with Satan and evil. The reason for his patronage of grocers is based upon his task of receiving risen souls and weighing them in his scales. His feast day, September 29, falls so close to the autumn equinox that early Christians renamed the original pagan holiday Michaelmas as a means of converting the heretics.

Milagros *(mee lah' gross)* Spanish origin. The name means miracle or astonishing vision. The name is bestowed in recognition of the miracles possible with faith in the Virgin María. The feast day for Nuestra Señora de los Milagros, Our Lady of Miracles, is held on July 9. Diminutive: Mili.

Milena *(mee lay' nah)* This name is a composition of the names Milagros (miracles) and Elena (light): hence the name means the light found in miracles.

Minerva *(mee nair' bah)* Latin origin. The name means wisdom, strength, or determination. She was the Roman goddess of education and the handiwork and skills involved with making crafts. Three saints bore this name.

Miranda *(mee rahn' dah)* Latin origin. Derived from *mirandus* (extraordinary, admirable).

Mireya *(mee ray' yah)* Hebrew origin. The name means God has spoken. Nine saints were bestowed with this name.

Monica *(mo' nee cah)* Latin origin. The name means monk. Other sources indicate the name means advisor, a definition that may have come from the most honored of saints bearing this name. St. Monica was an extremely devout mother who had great faith in her son, St. Augustine. Although he was leading a sinful life she followed him throughout his wanderings preaching the gospel the whole way. With the help of St. Ambrose she finally converted him to Christianity. One night mother and son discussed the bliss of the afterlife. Soon after, feeling her life's mission was complete, she died. St. Augustine went on to become one of the greatest theologians this world has ever known. Diminutive: Mona. Variation: Monika.

Natalia *(nah tah' lee ah)* Latin origin. Derived from *diēs nātālis* (natal day, Christmas). The name is customarily given to children who are born on Christmas Day. Diminutive: Talia.

Natividad *(nah tee bee dahd')* Latin origin. Derived from *natus* (born). Refers to the birth of Christ.

Nereida *(nay ray' dah)* Greek origin. Derived from *nēreid* (sea nymph). According to Greek mythology, there were fifty sea nymphs, daughters of the beloved sea god.

Nevara *(nay bah' rah)* Spanish origin. Derived from *nevar* (to snow). The name refers to the wholesomeness and purity of snow.

Nieves *(nee ay' bays)* Spanish origin. Derived from *nieves* (snows). The name is given in honor of the Virgin María, Nuestra Señora de las Nieves, Our Lady of Snows, which refers to a miracle of unmelted snow in hot weather.

Noemí *(no ay mee')* Hebrew origin. Derived from *nāomī* (my delight). The name also means beautiful, pleasant. Diminutive: Mimi. Variation: Noemé.

Obdulia *(obe doo' lee ah)* Latin origin. The name means she who lessens pain or sorrow. Diminutive: Lulu.

Octavia *(oak tah bee ah)* Latin origin. Derived from Octavius, a name that has its roots in *octavus* (eighth). The name appears eight times in the *Dictionary of Saints*.

Odilia *(o dee' lee ah)* Teutonic origin. The name is composed from the elements *od* (riches, wealth, prosperity) and *hild* (war, battle): hence the name means owner of many riches or prosperous through war. The name appears five times in the *Dictionary of Saints*. Diminutive: Tila. Variations: Odella, Othelia.

Olimpia *(o leem' pee ah)* Greek origin. Related to Olympus, a mountain in northern Greece and the mythological home of the gods.

Olivia *(oh lee' bee ah)* Latin origin. The name means olive tree. The olive tree signifies hope. It was a branch from this tree that the dove sent from Noah's ark returned with after forty days and forty nights of torrential floods, to let the survivors know they were now safe.

Ovelia *(o bay' lee ah)* Greek origin. Derived from *ōphelia* (helper): hence the name means she who provides relief.

Pacienca *(pah see enn' see ah)* Spanish origin. The name means patience.

Pacífica *(pah see' fee cah)* Latin origin. Female version of Pacífico. Derived from *pacificare* (to pacify, to make peace), a name that has its roots in *pax* (peace): hence the name has come to mean she who makes peace. Variation: Pacificia.

Paloma *(pah low' mah)* Spanish origin. The name means dove, the bird of peace.

Paola *(pow' lah)* Latin origin. Feminine form of Paulo. Derived from the Roman surname Paulus, which has its roots in *paulus* (small). A child is usually bestowed with this name in honor of St. Paulo, the first to preach Christ's gospel to the Gentile people. He was believed to be somewhat of a mystic, highly intelligent, and an untiring traveler. He is also revered as the patron saint of tentmakers. Variation: Paula.

Pascuala *(pahs kwall' lah)* Hebrew origin. Feminine equivalent to Pasqual. Derived from the Latin Paschālis (of Easter), which comes from Pascha (Easter), a word that has its roots in the Hebrew *pesach* (Passover). The name is customarily given to a child born during the Easter or Passover season. Variation: Pasquala.

Patricia *(pah tree' see ah)* Latin origin. Derived from *patricius* (a patrician, an aristocrat). Diminutive: Pati. Variations: Patriciana, Patrisa.

Pefilia *(pay fee' leee ah)* Spanish origin. Derived from *perfilar* (to outline, give shape, contour, or embellish).

Pentea *(pane tay' ah)* Unknown origin. Borrowed from a flower that belongs to the orchid family.

Perpetua *(pare pay' too ah)* Latin origin. Derived from *perpetus* (perpetual, continuous, and everlasting).

Petra *(pey trah)* Latin origin. Feminine form of Pedro. Derived from *petra* (rock or stone).

Petronilla *(pay tro nee' lah)* Latin origin. Derived from the Latin surname of Petronius, which has its roots in *petra* (rock or stone). Diminutive: Tona. Variations: Petrainilla, Petrolina.

Piedad *(pee ay dahd)* Spanish origin. The name means piety, goodness, holiness. Bestowing this name upon a child honors the Virgin María and Nuestra Señora de la Piedad, Our Lady of Piety.

Pilar *(pee lahr')* Spanish origin. The name means column, pillar. The name is given to pay tribute to the miracle of the Virgin María's astonishing appearance to Santiago over a marble pillar.

Preciosa *(pray see o' sah)* Spanish origin. The name means precious, cherished. The name is bestowed in reference to the precious blood of Christ.

Presencia *(pray sane' see ah)* Spanish origin. The name means presence. The name is bestowed upon a child to honor the awareness of Christ's presence during the Holy Communion, as well as the presence of God in all things, people, and situations.

Presentación *(pray sane tah see own')* Spanish origin. The name means presentation. The name refers to the presentation of Jesus Christ in the temple.

Prisciliana *(pree see lee ah nah)* Latin origin. Derived from the Roman surname of Priscus (ancient, old, or first). The name was borne by a first-century saint who was converted to Christianity by St. Pedro. Diminutive: Prex. Variations: Priceilla, Prisciana.

Pristina *(prees tee' nah)* Spanish origin. The name means pristine, fresh.

Prudencia *(proo dane' see ah)* Spanish origin. The name means prudence, caution. Diminutive: Pensita. Variations: Prudenciana, Prudintia.

Purificación *(poo ree fee kah' see own')* Spanish origin. The name means purification. The name is bestowed in honor of the ritual purification of the Blessed Mother, forty days after the birth of Christ. This ceremony is held on February 2. Diminutive: Puro. Variation: Puresa.

Purisima *(poo ree see mah)* Spanish origin. The name means the purest.

Rafaela *(rah fah ell' lah)* Hebrew origin. Feminine form of Rafael. Derived from *refāēl* (God has healed). The name was borne by one of the six archangels and the patron saint of travelers. Diminutives: Rafaelina, Raphaelita. Variations: Rafelia, Raphaela, Ravella.

Ramona *(rah mo' nah)* German origin. An arrangement of the elements *ragin* (counsel, wisdom) and *mund* (protection): hence the name means wise protection. Female form of Ramón or Raimundo. A girl is often bestowed with this name in dedication to St. Raimundo. St. Raimundo was born by cesarean section after his mother died during the birthing process—the basis for his surname (*non natus* meaning "not born") and his patronage and protection for childbirth. The souls of the women who die in childbirth are called the Ciauteteo (see-way-teh-tay-oh). After they give their life for their child they become angels that meet the sun at the zenith and guide it to the horizon. Legend has it that if it weren't for these beautiful martyrs the sun would never rest. Diminutives: Mona, Monona. Variations: Ramoina, Ramonelia.

Raquel *(rah kel')* Hebrew origin. Derived from *rāhēl* (ewe or sheep). A ewe is the symbol of gentleness and purity. In the Bible she was the beloved wife of Jacob, mother of Joseph and Benjamin. Diminutives: Quelita, Raco. Variations: Racheal, Rochel.

Rebeca *(ray bay' kah)* Hebrew origin. Derived from *ribbqāh* (noose): hence the name has come to mean to tie or bind. Another source offers beautiful as an alternative meaning. In the Bible, she was the strong-willed wife of Isaac, as well as the mother of Jacob and Esau. Two saints bore this name. Diminutives: Bequi, Bequita. Variations: Rebekah, Reveca.

Refugio *(ray foo' hee oh)* Latin origin. The name means refuge, a place of safety and protection. The name is bestowed in honor of the protection of the Blessed Mother, hence Nuestra Señora del Refugio, Our Lady of Refuge. Diminutives: Cuco, Refugito. Variations: Refigio, Refutio.

Regina *(ray hee' nah)* Latin origin. The name means ruler, royalty, queen, or queenly. It is also the official title of a reigning queen. The name appears five times in the *Dictionary of Saints*. It also refers to the oldest psalm, Hail Holy Queen. Diminutive: Gina. Variations: Aregina, Reina, Rejinia.

Remedio *(ray may' dee oh)* Latin origin. The name means remedy, medicine, and solutions or answers. Bestowing this name pays homage to the trust that all answers will be revealed and problems remedied with faith in the Virgin María. Several churches utilize this attribute of the Blessed Mother in the name of their church, such as Nuestra Señora de los Remedios, Our Lady of Remedies. One such church in Mexico displays an image of the Blessed Mother brought from Spain during the conquest.

Ricarda *(ree kar' dah)* Anglo-Saxon origin. Female form of Ricardo. The name combines the elements *rik* (ruler, king) and *hart* (strong, brave): hence the name means a strong king. There are nineteen saints mentioned in the *Dictionary of Saints*. Diminutive: Rica. Variations: Recharda, Ricardeta, Ricarla.

Rita *(ree' tah)* Greek origin. Although the name is derived from Margarita (pearl) it is often bestowed as a separate given name. The fifteenth-century patron saint of desperate causes, marital problems, and parenthood bore this name. For the last fifteen years of her life she suffered from wounds on her head that appeared as if she had worn a crown of thorns.

Rosa *(ro' sah)* Latin origin. The name means rose. St. Rosa of Lima was the first American to be canonized. Her devotion to her family is highly regarded. She spent all her hours growing flowers and doing embroidery to support the family. She later led an isolated life, wore a circlet studded with thorns, and took tremendous care of the poor, slaves, sick, and Peruvian Indians. This name is often used in combination with several other names. Diminutives: Chita, Rosi, Rosita. Variations: Rosado, Rosember.

Rosabel *(roe sah bell')* Combination of Rosa (rose) and Bella (beautiful): hence the name means beautiful rose.

Rosalba *(roe sahl' bah)* Combination of Rosa (rose) and Alba (white): hence the name means white rose.

Rosalia *(roe sah lee ah)* Latin origin. The name is given in honor of the annual Roman tradition of placing roses on the graves or tombs of loved ones. Diminutives: Chala, Lía. Variations: Rosaelia, Rosalya.

Rosalinda *(roe sah leen' dah)* Combination of Rosa (rose) and Linda (pretty): hence the name means pretty rose. Other sources say it may be of Germanic origin with the compounding of the elements *hrôs* (fame, reputation) and *lind* (gentle, tender): hence in this way the name means known for her gentle ways. Diminutive: Lina. Variation: Roselín.

Rosamunda *(roe sah moon' dah)* Combination of Rosa (rose) and *mundo* (world): hence the name means rose of the world.

Rosana *(roe sah' nah)* Combination of Rosa (rose) and Ana (graceful): hence the name means graceful, refined as a rose. Variation: Rosania.

Rosario *(roe sah' ree oh)* Latin origin. The name means a bed of roses or a rose garden. It refers to the rosary and devotional prayers to the Virgin María. The name can also be given in honor of Nuestra Señora del Rosario, Our Lady of the Rosary.

Rosaura *(roe saow rah)* Combination of Rosa (rose) and Aurelia or aurea (gold): hence the name means rose of gold. Variation: Rosarra.

Sabina *(sah bee' nah)* Latin origin. The name means born in Sabina. The Sabines were an ancient people living in central Italy. They were conquered by the Romans in the third century B.C.

Samjuana *(sam hwahn' ah)* Combination of Samuel (his name is God) and Juana (God is gracious): hence the name means by his name we know God is gracious.

Sanjuana *(sahn hwahn' ah)* Combination of *san* (saint) and Juana (God is gracious): hence the name means a saint by God's grace.

Santana *(sahn tah' nah)* Combination of *san* (saint) and Ana (gracious, merciful): hence the name means gracious saint.

Sara *(sah rah)* Hebrew origin. Derived from *sārāh* (princess). In the Bible, she was the wife of Abraham. At ninety she gave birth to Isaac. Diminutives: Chara, Sarita. Variations: Sahra, Sares, Sera.

Seferina *(say fay ree' no)* Latin origin. Female version of Ceferino. The name means gentle breeze. Some believe the name has its roots in *sĕrāphīm* (seraphim, the burning ones, or angels who surround God's throne), a word that has its roots in *sāraph* (to burn). Diminutives: Cefia, Rina, Sefia. Variations: Ceferina, Sefriana, Zeferna.

Serena *(say ray' nah)* Latin origin. The name means serene, tranquil, calm. Twelve saints bore this beautiful name. Variation: Syrina.

Silvana *(seel bah' nah)* Latin origin. Feminine variant of Silvano. Derived from the surname Silvānus (of the woods), a name that has its roots in *silva* (woods, forest). The name also has its roots in Silvanus, the Roman god of woods and fields. He can be invoked to protect the boundaries of fields from invaders. The name appears forty-two times in the *Dictionary of Saints*. Variation: Silvera.

Silvia *(seel bee' ah)* Latin origin. Feminine variant of Silvano. Derived from the surname Silvānus (of the woods), a name that has its roots in *silva* (woods, forest).

Simplicia *(seem plee' see ah)* Latin origin. Derived from Simplicius, which has its roots in *simplex* (simple, uncomplicated). The name appears twenty-one times in the *Dictionary of Saints*. Variations: Simplicitas, Siplicia.

Socorra *(so ko' rah)* Spanish origin. The name is derived from Socorro (help, assistance). It is also given in honor of the Virgin María and Nuestra Señora del Perpetuo Socorro, Our Lady of Perpetual Help. Diminutive: Cocó. Variations: Socaria, Socorio.

Sofía *(so fee' ah)* Greek origin. Derived from *sophia* (wisdom, skill). Eighteen saints bore this name. Diminutives: Chofi, Fia, Soficita. Variations: Sofi, Sonia.

Solana *(so lah nah)* Latin origin. The name means sunshine.

Soledad *(so lay dahd')* Spanish origin. The name means
solitude. The name is given in honor of the Virgin
María and Nuestra Señora de la Soledad, Our Lady of
Solitude. Diminutive: Cholita. Variations: Soladá, So-
lidera.

Spirita *(spee ree' tah)* Latin origin. The name means
spirit. It refers to the Holy Spirit, the third member of
the Trinity.

Susana *(soo sah' nah)* Hebrew origin. Derived from
shōshannāh (lily). The name is borne in the Bible by
a follower and caretaker of Jesus Christ. Sixteen saints
are mentioned in the *Dictionary of Saints*. Diminutives:
Susi, Susy. Variations: Suzanna, Zuzana.

Tabita *(tah bee' tah)* Aramaic origin. The name means
gazelle, a swift graceful antelope from Africa.

Tamara *(tah mah' rah)* Hebrew origin. The name means
she who provides an amiable or pleasant refuge.

Teodora *(tay o dor ah)* Greek origin. Female version of
Teodoro. The name is a combination of *theos* (God)
and *dōron* (gift): hence the name means gift of God.
One hundred and forty-six saints bore this name. Diminutive: Doya. Variations: Teodara, Tiodoria.

Teresa *(tay ray' sah)* Greek origin. The name means of
Tharasia or it may be construed to have originated from
terizein (to reap or gather). There are two extraordinary
women of the church that carried the name Teresa. St.
Teresa of Avila and St. Thérèse of Lisieux were quite
different in their devotion to God and church. Teresa
of Avila was a nun of the Carmelite Order and worked
with St. John of the Cross to reform this sector of the
church. The first woman to be honored as a Doctor of
the Church, she was a skilled cook and commanded
her fellow sisters with a strict hand. By contrast, St.
Thérèse of Lisieux led a more plain life. She cultivated

and perfected simplicity and humility and ordinariness in her autobiography *The Story of a Soul*. She suffered from tuberculosis and offered her painful steps each day to missionaries and ship pilots, hence she became their patron saint. Diminutives: Tea, Teresita, Tessa. Variations: Terasa, Thérèse, Tresa.

Tomasa *(toe mahs' ah)* Aramaic origin. The name means a twin. Girls christened thusly are often named after St. Tomás. Tomás was an apostle and remembered as Doubting Tomás because he refused to believe in the risen Christ until he touched his wounds. When the dawn of belief and faith came over him he proclaimed, "My Lord and my God!" (John 20: 28), which has since become a powerful meditation prayer. Tomás is the patron saint of architects because of a characteristic legend of his life and disposition. Tomás was granted a large sum of money to construct a palace, for which he had the plans. Instead Tomás symbolically built "a palace in heaven" by spending the money on the poor. Diminutive: Tomasita. Variations: Tamasa, Tomasina.

Tonantzin *(toe nahn' see in)* Aztec origin. She is the Aztec goddess of earth and corn, but is also known as virgin and little mother. Her shrine was constructed upon Tepeyac Hill, near the modern-day capital Mexico City. During the Spanish conquest the natives mourned her loss so deeply that when the dark-skinned Virgin of Guadalupe appeared at their goddess's sacred sight to one of their own people they embraced her with ardent reverence.

Tránsito *(trahn' see toe)* Latin origin. The name means transfer, or passage. The name refers to the inevitable transfer of Virgin María's soul from earth to heaven after her death. Diminutive: Tacho. Variation: Tráncito.

Tresiliana *(tray see lee ah' nah)* Spanish origin. Derived from *tres* (three). Often the third child is bestowed with this name.

Tulia *(too' lee ah)* Latin origin. The name means she who has risen from the ground. Variation: Tuliana.

Úrsula *(oor' soo lah)* Latin origin. Derived from *ursa* (she-bear): hence the name means little she-bear. Bear represents the power of introspection. According to Native American thought, the bear hibernates in her cave for the winter months. It is here she digests the year's events and attunes herself to the safety of the connection with Mother Earth. We can call on the strength of the bear to aid us in our search for the truth by quieting, for it is in the silence that we will find our answers. The constellations Ursa Major and Ursa Minor, also known as the Big and Little Dipper, can be found in the skies of the northern hemisphere throughout most of the year. Of the fifteen saints who bore this name the most famous was a fourth-century saint who refused to marry the king of the Huns and was martyred with eleven thousand of her companions.

Veneranda *(bay nah rahn' dah)* Latin origin. Derived from *venerando* (venerable, worthy of admiration, respect, and honor). Seven saints bore this name.

Verónica *(bay ro' nee kah)* Latin origin. Derived from the elements *vera* (true) and *icon* (image): hence the name means a true image. This definition originated from an anagram of *vera icon,* which translated means a true image. Veronica is remembered as the compassionate woman who wiped the sweaty and bloody brow of Jesus Christ on his way to crucifixion. As a miraculous reward for her kind gesture, Jesus' features were imprinted on the woman's handkerchief. Diminutive: Roni. Variation: Varónica.

Victoria *(beek' tor ee ah)* Latin origin. The name means victory. Diminutives: Lina, Toya, Viqui. Variations: Victorina, Viktoriana.

Vincenta *(bee sane' tah)* Latin origin. Vincenta is the female version of Vincent. Related to *vincere* (to conquer). Sixty-one saints bore this name, including Vincente of Saragossa, one of the most illustrious martyrs from Spain. Diminutives: Vicinta, Visenta.

Viola *(bee oh' lah)* Latin origin. The name means violet. A flower from this family may have white, blue, purple, or yellow petals. According to mythology these precious flowers were said to have originally sprung from the tears of the goddess Isis. They have been used medicinally as an antiseptic, to soothe sore throats, and as an aphrodisiac. They are also edible and have been added to syrups, jellies, and other desserts. Variation: Violeta.

Virginia *(beer hee' nee ah)* Latin origin. The name relates to virgin and means pure, chaste. Diminutive: Gina. Variation: Virgena.

Virtudes *(beer too' days)* Latin origin. The name means virtuous and refers to the three virtues of faith, hope, and charity. Also connected to the angels that God sends forth to conduct miracles here on earth.

Vivian *(bee bee ahn')* Latin origin. Derived from *vivus* (alive). Baptized Vivia, Perpetua was a Roman martyr, who became St. Perpetua. She experienced several remarkable visions in which she conquered the devil. Diminutive: Bibi. Variations: Bibiana, Vivia.

Wanda *(wahn' dah)* Teutonic origin. The name means wanderer.

Xochil *(sho' cheel)* Aztec origin. The name means where the flowers abound. Of all the Native American names being used this one is the most popular.

Xochiquetzal *(sho chee ket' sal)* Aztec origin. The name means feather flower, possibly related to the soft, feathery petals of the goddess's sacred flower, the yellow marigold. She is the goddess of dance, music, crafts, and love. According to Aztec mythology, a great flood destroyed everyone except Xochiquetzal and one mortal man. Together they populated the earth. It is believed all the different languages and races arose from the children of these parents. For this reason she is also known as the mother of the world.

Yemena *(yay man' ah)* Cuban origin. According to the Cuban pantheon she is the divine mother of all fourteen gods and goddesses. She is the great goddess of the ocean and motherhood since it is from the sea that all humankind and animals are born. She is revered as the Holy Queen Sea.

Yolanda *(yo lahn' dah)* Greek origin. The name means pretty as a violet. Diminutive: Yola. Variations: Jolanda, Ylonda.

Zenaida *(zay nay' dah)* Greek origin. The name means pertaining to Zeus, the patriarch of Greek mythology. Diminutive: Naida. Variations: Seneida, Zenoida.

Zita *(zee' tah)* Hebrew origin. The name means mistress. The name is also believed to be a pet form of Rosita, hence the meaning would be little rose. A thirteenth-century saint by this name is the patroness of domestic servants.

Zoé *(zo ā')* Greek origin. The name means life.

Zolia *(zoy' lah)* Greek origin. Derived from *zoé* (life).

Zoraida *(zo rye' dah)* Arabic origin. The name means captivating woman. The name gained notoriety from characters in the operas *Zoraida di Granata* and *Don Quixote*.

Zuleica (*zoo lay' kah*) Arabic origin. Derived from *zu-leika* (fair).

Zulema (*zoo lay' mah*) Hebrew origin. The name means peace. Diminutives: Suly, Zula. Variations: Solemna, Zulerma.

Boys' Names A–Z

Abacum (*ah bah coom'*) Unknown origin. He was a third-century saint who was martyred for ministering to Christians.

Abán (*ah bahn'*) Arabic origin. This name comes from Persian mythology. He was a muse of liberal arts and mechanics.

Abaristo (*ah bah rees' toe*) Greek origin. In modern translation the word has come to mean agreeable. Variations: Avaristo, Avarsito.

Abdalah (*ahb dah' yah*) Arabic origin. The name means servant of God. Variation: Abdullah.

Abdénago (*ahb day' nah go*) Hebrew origin. The name comes from Abédnego, meaning servant of the god Nego. In the Bible, King Nebuchadnezzar threw Abenago, along with his companions Shadrach and Meshach, into the fiery pit because they refused to worship a golden image. When the king's men looked into the pit they saw four men walking around. They ordered the men to come out of the fire. They came out unscathed with not a hint of smoke on them. The fourth man was believed to be an angel of the one true God. Variations: Abdeniago, Abedmago, Adbonego, Avendio.

Abdías (*ahb dee' ahs*) Hebrew origin. The name means slave of God. He is also remembered as a saint who in 900 B.C. foretold of the destruction of Edom.

Abdiel *(ahb deal')* Hebrew origin. This name also means servant of God. In the Bible Abdiel was the prophet who withstood Satan.

Abdón *(ahb doan')* Semitic origin. The meaning of this name is servant of God. Recently the name has changed somewhat to mean little servant. He is remembered as a third-century Roman saint. Diminutive: Nona. Variations: Abdó, Abedón.

Abdulia *(ahb doo' lee ah)* Arabic origin. The literal translation is servant of Allah.

Abejundio *(ah bay hoon' dee oh)* Spanish origin. The name derives from the *abeja,* or bee. Variation: Abejundo.

Abel *(ah bell')* Hebrew origin. The name is derived from the Hebrew word *hebel* (breath). The modern sense of the word is breath of vanity. In the Bible, Abel was the second son of Adam and Eve. Variations: Abelon, Abiel, Avel.

Abelardo *(ah bay lahr' doe)* Teutonic origin. This name is a combination of *adel* (noble) and *hard* (brave, strong, hardy): hence the meaning is nobly steadfast and determined. A variation of this name was used as a surname for Peter Abelard's love for Heloise in a great romance of medieval France. Diminutives: Beluch, Lalo. Variations: Afelardo, Avelardo, Ebelardo, Evilardo.

Abelino *(ah bay lee' no)* Spanish origin. The name derives from *avellanos* (hazelnut trees) or finds its origins from the city of Avellino, place of hazelnut trees. Variations: Avalino, Avelimo, Avellino, Obelino.

Abil *(ah beel')* Latin origin. Derived from the word *asella* (beautiful). Variations: Abilio, Aviel.

Abimael *(ah bee my el')* Hebrew origin. The name means father of God.

Abimelech *(ah bee may' leck)* Hebrew origin. The name means father is king. In the Bible, Abimelech was a Canaanite king who took Sarah into his harem.

Abirio *(ah bee' ree oh)* Hebrew origin. The name means father is exalted. According to the Bible he rebelled against Moses and Aaron and was later swallowed by the earth.

Abraham *(ah brah ahm')* Hebrew origin. The name means exalted father, father of a mighty nation, or father of the multitude. Abraham is praised as the patriarch, father, and founder of the Jewish and Arab tribes. He was the first to illustrate great loyalty and faith in God. Diminutive: Brancho. Variations: Aberhan, Ahbrán, Avrán, Habrán, Ibrahim.

Absalón *(ahb sah lone')* Hebrew origin. The name means father of peace. In the Bible, he was the rebellious yet favorite son of David. Absalón is remembered for his long hair and great beauty.

Abundio *(ah boon' dee oh)* Latin origin. The name is related to the word *abundius*, which has its roots in *abundas* (abundant, copious, plenty). In modern translation, the name means full of good works. Diminutive: Abundito. Variations: Abondio, Aboundio, Abundancio, Abundencio.

Acacio *(ah cah' see oh)* Greek origin. It is derived from the Greek word *akakia* (acacia tree, a thorny tree). In modern translation, the name has come to mean honorable. Variations: Acarcius, Accasius, Alcasio, Anicacio, Ecasio.

Aciano *(ah see ah' no)* Spanish origin. The name originates from the blue bottle flower.

Acilino *(ah see lee' no)* Latin origin. The name derives from the Latin word *aquila,* meaning like an eagle.

Thirteen saints were christened with this name. Variations: Acilnio, Ancilino, Aquilino.

Acisclo *(ah sees' cloe)* Latin origin. It is related to the word *acisculus* (an instrument for shaping stones). It is also the name of a fourth-century saint who was martyred at Cordova. His feast day is November 1.

Adalbaldo *(ah dahl ball' doe)* German origin. The name combines *adal* (of noble lineage) with *baldo* (to fight). The composition of the name translates to mean the fight of the nobility.

Adalberto *(ah dahl bare' toe)* German origin. The name combines *adal* (of noble lineage) with *beraht* (bright or resplendent). This arrangement means bright nobility. A saint by this name, born in the tenth century, is the patron saint of Bohemia and Poland. His feast day is April 23. Diminutives: Adal, Beto. Variations: Adalverto, Addiberto, Adelberto, Adialberto, Edilberto.

Adalrico *(ah dahl ree co')* German origin. The name combines *adal* (of noble lineage) with *rik* (ruler, boss). Put together, the name translates to the boss of the nobility.

Adalvino *(ah dahl bee no')* German origin. The name combines *adal* (of noble lineage) with *win* (friend). The whole name means a noble friend or a friend of the nobility.

Adán *(ah dahn')* Hebrew origin. The name literally means red earth. This connection to nature identifies the essence of man, and our mirror image of God. Five saints were given this name. Variation: Adanaton.

Adauco *(ah dowk' toe)* Latin origin. It is related to the word *adauctus,* meaning to increase or grow. This was also the name of a fourth-century saint. His feast day is February 7. Variations: Adauco, Adauto.

Adelfo *(ah dell' foe)* Greek origin. The name means from the same form and is also translated to mean brother or sibling. Variations: Adelphino, Adelfino, Adelphuna, Odelfo, Odelfio, Odelfina.

Adelmo *(ah dell' mo)* German origin. Derived from a combination of the elements *adal* (noble) and *mund* (protection): hence the arrangement means noble protector. The name was borne by an eighth-century English saint, whose feast day is May 25. Diminutives: Delma, Delmo. Variations: Adelelmo, Adelman, Adelnery.

Ademar *(ah day mar')* German origin. The name comes from the name Hadumar, which combines *hild* (combate, battle) with *mers* (illustrious, brilliant, and famous). Therefore the name means legendary in battle or famous, illustrious, brilliant in combat. Variations: Ademaro, Adimaro.

Adeodato *(ah day oh dah' toe)* Latin origin. The name means one given to God.

Adolfo *(ah dole' fo)* German origin. The name combines the elements *adal* (noble) with *wulf* (wolf): hence the name means noble wolf or even noble hero. He was a thirteenth-century German bishop whose feast day is February 11. Diminutives: Dolfito, Dolfo, Fonso. Variations: Adulfo, Ydolfo.

Adón *(ah doan')* Phoenician origin. The name means Lord. Possibly a Hebrew name for God. Variation: Adonino.

Adonaldo *(ah doe nahl' doe)* Spanish origin. The name means full of ability.

Adonías *(ah doe nee' ahs)* Hebrew origin. The name means Jehovah is Lord. The name was borne in the Bible by David's fourth son who attempted to succeed his father. Variations: Adonais, Adonaiso.

Adonís *(ah doe nees')* Phoenician origin. The name means Lord. Because he was the male god of beauty in Greek mythology, the name has also come to mean handsome or good-looking.

Adrián *(ah dree ahn')* Latin origin. Derived from the Latin surname of Adriānus (man from the city of Adria).

Adulio *(ah dyoo' lee oh)* Latin origin. The name means compulsive urge to please.

Aemilio *(ah mee' lee oh)* Latin origin. Derived from the Roman surname of Aemilius, which has its roots in *aemulus* (rival, to compete or emulate). Variation: Aemiliano.

Agustino *(ah goos tee' no)* Latin origin. Derived from the Latin *augustus,* meaning revered, majestic, dignified, or exalted. Diminutives: Asta, Cacho, Chucho, Tino, Tito, Tuto. Variations: Agostín, Augustavo, Augustín, Augusto, Austeo.

Aladino *(ah lah de' no)* Arabic origin. The name means height of religion. The name is a compound of the words *a'lā* (height), *al* (the), and *dīn* (religion). In literature he was the hero of *Arabian Nights* and of a Disney animated feature film.

Alamar *(ah lah mar')* Arabian origin. The name means an adornment of gold, golden, or covered in gold. Variation: Alamaro.

Alano *(ah ian' oh)* Celtic origin. The name means fair and handsome. Two saints were bestowed with this name.

Alaríco *(ah lah ree' co)* Teutonic origin. Derived from the German Adalrich, which combines the elements *adal* (noble) with *rik* (ruler, king). The arrangement means ruler of all or noble ruler. A Visigothic king by this name pillaged Rome in 400 A.D. Diminutive: Rico.

Albano *(ahl bah' no)* Latin origin. The name derives from the Latin *albus* (white). There are four saints christened with this name. Variation: Albanasius.

Albaro *(ahl' bah roe)* German origin. The name means altogether cautious or extremely careful. In another sense, the name finds its roots in the Old English Æfhere. This name combines the elements *æf* (elf) and *here* (army): hence the arrangement means elfin army. Three saints have this name. Diminutives: Alvi and Lalo. Variations: Alvar, Alvaro, Alverico.

Alberto *(ahl bare' toe)* German origin. The name combines *al* (noble) with *beraht* (bright or glorious): hence the name means of glorious nobility. Although there were twenty-eight saints with this name, the most well known, St. Alberto, was one of the most astute and highly evolved scientists of the thirteenth century. He devoted himself to writing books about astronomy and geography, logic and mathematics, physics and chemistry, and the natural sciences and philosophy, as well as theology and ethics.

Alcibíades *(ahl see bee' ah days)* Greek origin. The name means one who lives a vigorous life. Children bestowed with this name have the qualities of being dynamic and energetic inherent in their name.

Aldegundo *(ahl day goon' doe)* German origin. The name is derived from the combination of *adal* (noble) with *hild* (battle), hence the battle of nobility. A variation of this name, Aldegundis, was a third-century saint. Variations: Aldonza, Aldegundis.

Aldo *(ahl' doe)* German origin. The name means noble. In another sense of the word the name indicates broad or extensive experience. The name is listed twice in the *Dictionary of Saints.*

Aleatero *(ah lay ah tay' roe)* Spanish origin. The name means dependent upon good fortune.

Alejandro *(ah lay hahn' droe)* Greek origin. The name means defender of men or he who protects men. The meaning of this name comes from the combination of *alexein* (to defend or help) with *andros* (man). Alejandro was one of the greatest generals of all time, conquering much of the ancient world. Of all the forty-six saints with the name Alejandro, the best known was a fifth-century saint, who performed many miracles. Diminutives: Alejo, Alendro, Alex, Jeandro. Variations: Alasio, Alefandro, Alejandor, Elisandro.

Alentín *(ah lain teen')* Spanish origin. The name means one who inspires or encourages.

Alfonso *(ahl fone' so)* German origin. The name means noble and ready. It combines the German word *adal* (noble) with *funs* (ready, prompt, able). Many saints had this given name. Diminutives: Foncho, Loncho. Variations: Alefonso, Alfegio, Alonso, Alphone.

Alfredo *(ahl fray doe')* Anglo-Saxon origin. Derived from the Spanish Alfred, which combines the words *ælf* (elf) with *ræd* (council): hence the name means elfin council. In Old England, elves were considered clairvoyant, sagacious, and wise. The villagers would venture to the wilds and consult the "little people" who could see into the future and decipher the outcome of events before they unfolded. Therefore the name has come to mean wise council. San Alfredo was a fourth-century saint. Diminutive: Fredo. Variations: Alfedo, Elfridio.

Alicio *(ah lee' see oh)* Greek origin. In the Greek language the name means truth. The German variation of the name signifies helper or protector. Some believe the name is derived from the German *alexien* (to defend or come to one's aid). A thirteenth-century saint was bestowed with this name. Diminutive: Chichi. Variations: Aliceto, Aliseo.

Alipio *(ah lee' pee oh)* Greek origin. The name means he who is void of sadness or strife. He was a seventh-century saint.

Alirio *(ah lee' ree oh)* He was a French saint in the fourth century.

Almaquio *(ahl mock' key oh)* A Roman of this name was a fourth-century saint who was martyred for protesting gladiator sports.

Aloisio *(ah low ee' see oh)* German origin. Derived from Hloudowig, which combines the elements *hloud* (famous or glorious) with *wīg* (war). The combination means famous or glorious in war. San Aloysius Gonzaga is the patron saint of the youth. Variations: Aloysius, Luis.

Amadeo *(ah may day' oh)* Latin origin. The name is derived from *amor* (love) and means he who loves God. He was a fifteenth-century saint. Variations: Amades, Amado.

Amaranto *(ah mah rahn' toe)* Latin origin. The name means imperishable. A third-century saint bore this name. Diminutives: Amario, Emaro. Variations: Amarande, Amerardo.

Amasio *(ah mah' see oh)* Latin origin. The name means lover. Variation: Amachio.

Ambrosio *(ahm bro' see oh)* Greek origin. Derived from the Greek *ambrosios* (immortal). Since the Greek pantheon was considered to be immortal as well, the name has come to mean relating to the gods. The fourth-century saint who bore this name was a bishop and honored as one of the four greatest Latin Doctors of the Church. Diminutives: Bocho, Locho, Pocho. Variations: Ambarosio, Ambraso, Ambrose.

Américo *(ah may' ree co)* German origin. This name is
a Spanish equivalent of the Italian Enrico, which gets
its roots from the German Heinrich (ruler of an enclo-
sure or home ruler). Amerigo Vespucci was an explorer
who discovered the Americas. Diminutives: Merco,
Mimeco.

Amós *(ah mohs')* Hebrew origin. Derived from *āmōs*
(fated to be burdened or troubled). The name was
borne by a biblical prophet whose predictions of the
disaster of Israel appear in the Old Testament book of
Amos.

Amparo *(ahm pah' roe)* Spanish origin. The name
means favored or protected. Variations: Amparao, Em-
paro.

Ampelio *(ahm pay' lee oh)* Greek origin. The name
means cultivator of vines.

Anacleto *(ah nah clay' toe)* Greek origin. Derived from
the Greek *anaklētos* (called forth, invoked loudly). A
second-century martyr bore this name. Diminutives:
Amacleto, Ancleto, Naclito. Variations: Anaclitor,
Cleto, Enicleto.

Ananías *(ah nah nee' ahs)* Hebrew origin. The name
means God is merciful. In the Bible, God appeared to
a holy man from Damascus who bore this name.

Anastacio *(ah nah stah' see oh)* Greek origin. Derived
from the Greek *anastasis* (resurrection). Many saints
bore this name. Diminutives: Anasto, Nancho, Tachito.
Variations: Anacasio, Anastasíum, Anstaceo, Atansio.

Anatolio *(ah nah toe' lee oh)* Greek origin. The name
means one who comes from the east. Current translations of the name have modified it to symbolize daybreak, sunrise, or dawn, even an awakening. Variations
of this name appear four times in the *Dictionary of
Saints*. Variations: Anastolio, Antolín.

Andrés *(ahn drays')* Greek origin. The name means strong or manly. Modern alterations have transformed the name to mean "the virile one." Andrés was one of Christ's first apostles. He was called from his fishing nets by Jesus and asked to become a fisher of men. He was martyred on an X-shaped cross. Diminutives: Andy, Necho, Tito. Variations: Andero, Andreolo, Ondés.

Angel *(ahn' hell)* Greek origin. The name means messenger or thoughts from God. Angels are seen as spiritual beings who pass messages to humans and are perceived as inspirations of purity, goodness, and safety. Many Christians call upon their angels for guidance and protection.

Aniseto *(ah nee say' toe)* Greek origin. The name means invincible. Two saints bore this name.

Ansberto *(ahns bair' toe)* German origin. The name is a combination of the elements *ansi* (divinity, related to God) and *beraht* (bright, or splendor): hence the combination means the splendor of God. Variations: Esverda.

Anselmo *(ahn sell' mo)* German origin. The name is a combination of the elements *ansi* (divinity, related to God) with *helm* (helmet, protection): hence the name means protected by God. There were many saints with this name. Diminutives: Semo, Yemo. Variations: Anselino, Auselm, Zelmo.

Antonio *(ahn toe' nee oh)* Latin origin. The name means beyond price or precious. Of the many St. Antonios listed in the *Dictionary of Saints,* St. Antonio of Padua's exceptional talent for preaching and teaching made him one of the most well known. He is remembered as an indefatigable man of great intelligence. He was a Franciscan friar who held immense compassion for the poor. One of the twenty-one California missions was named after this beloved saint on July 14, 1771. Diminutives: Antonieto, Antonulo, Tonio, Tony. Variations: Andón, Antonius, Natonio.

Anunciación *(ah noon' see ah see own')* Spanish origin. The name means to announce and refers to Gabriel's announcement to Mary that she would give birth to the Christ child. A feast day of March 25 is dedicated to honor this event known as the Annunciation. Diminutive: Anuncio. Variation: Nuncio.

Aparicio *(ah pah ree' see oh)* Spanish origin. The name means the act of appearing and refers to Jesus Christ's appearance after his resurrection. Variation: Aparición.

Apolo *(ah poe' low)* Greek origin. The name means of the sun's power. In Greek mythology he was the sun god in addition to the deity of music, poetry, prophesy, medicine, and pastoral activities. He is also known for his great beauty. There are many saints bestowed with this name, including an early Christian man who taught in the land of Alejandria. Variation: Apolo.

Apolonio *(ah po low' nee oh)* Greek origin. The name means the light from the sun. Variations of this given name appear several times in the *Dictionary of Saints.* Diminutives: Loño, Poli. Variations: Apolinar, Apolinario, Polinarius.

Aquiles *(ah key' lace).* Greek origin. The name means without lips. In Greek mythology, Aquiles was a great war hero and leader whose only weak spot was his ankles. Aquilo was an early follower of Jesus Christ. He and his wife Priscilla met Paul at Corinth. Diminutive: Quilo. Variation: Aquilo.

Aquilino *(ah key lee' no)* Latin origin. The name means like an eagle. This name appears several times in the *Dictionary of Saints.*

Arcadio *(ahr cah' dee oh)* Greek origin. The name means one born in Arcadia. Diminutive: Cadio. Variations: Acadro, Arcadie, Arcodyo.

Ariano *(ah ree ah' no)* Greek origin. The name means warlike. In the Greek pantheon he was equivalent to the Roman Mars, god of war. Variation: Arrio.

Aristeo *(ah rees tay' oh)* Greek origin. The name is derived from the Greek *aristos* (best). Other interpretations consider the name to mean one who is inflexible. A second-century saint bore this name. Variations: Aresteo, Aristedes.

Armando *(ahr mahn doe)* German origin. This name combines the German elements *heri* (army) and *man* (man): hence the arrangement means a soldier or warrior. It is also interpreted to denote a hero of the army. Diminutive: Mando. Variations: Almando, Arminio, Armundo, German.

Arno *(ar no)* German origin. This name is derived from the German *arn* (eagle). According to Native American spirituality the eagle will help us with our connection to the divine. The eagle represents the state of grace and personal power that is achieved after hard work. Variation: Arnel.

Arnoldo *(ahr nol doe)* German origin. This name combines the German elements *arn* (eagle) and *wald* (power or strength): hence the combination means strong or as powerful as an eagle. A ninth-century German saint who bore this name is remembered for his devotion to the poor. Variations: Armaldo, Ornaldo.

Arnulfo *(are null' fo)* German origin. This name combines the German elements *arn* (eagle) and *wulf* (wolf). Many saints bore his name. Diminutive: Nulfo. Variations: Amulfo, Arnulio, Ernolfo.

Aron *(ah roan')* Egyptian origin. Derived from the Hebrew *aharón* (the exalted one). Today's meaning is translated to the enlightened one. He was the brother of Moses and first high priest of the Jews. In the Hebrew language it has a variety of meanings including light, inspiration, teaching, singing, shining, and mountain. Variations: Aronida, Arrón, Erón.

Arquímedes *(are kee' may dees)* Latin origin. This name combines the German elements *archi* (chief, first, lead) and *mēdesthai* (to meditate or contemplate): hence the combination means the first to think about something. Current interpretation translates the word to mean inventor or originator. An important third-century B.C. Greek mathematician, physician, and inventor bore this name.

Arsenio *(are say' nee oh)* Greek origin. Derived from the Greek *arsenio* (male, virile, masculine). There are fourteen saints by this name in the *Dictionary of Saints.*

Artemio *(are tay' mee oh)* Greek origin. The name means whole and perfect. There are eleven saints by this name in the *Dictionary of Saints.* Diminutive: Micha. Variations: Aretimo, Hortemio, Otemio.

Arturo *(are too' ro)* Celtic origin. The name means noble on high. Diminutives: Pituro, Turi. Variations: Alturo, Auturo.

Aselo *(ah say' low)* Latin origin. The name is believed to have derived from the Latin *asinus* (little donkey or burro). Another source states the name means slender ash tree.

Asterio *(ahs tay' ree oh)* Latin origin. The name means shines like a star. In Greek mythology, Zeus turned him into a quail. This name appears eleven times in the *Dictionary of Saints.*

Asuncion *(ah soon see own')* Latin origin. Derived from the Spanish *asunción* (assumption) and refers to the taking of the Virgin María's body from earth to heaven, celebrated as the Assumption. Many saints of both genders were bestowed with this name. Diminutives: Acencio, Chencho. Variations: Ansencio, Ascendión, Aucenisio.

Atanasio *(ah tah nah' see oh)* Greek origin. Derived from the Greek *athanasia* (immortality or without death, living eternally). A fourth-century scholar by this name is honored for his fight against Arian heresy. Diminutive: Tanacio. Variations: Adamacio, Athanasius, Tunacio.

Atreo *(ah tray' oh)* Derived from the Greek Atreus. In Greek mythology, the relationships and events of the Atreus family served as inspiration for many Greek tragedies.

Audífaz *(ow dee' faz)* Latin origin. The name means one who instigates an attack. He was a second-century martyr who was killed for trying to consecrate the remains of other slain martyrs.

Aurelio *(ow ray' lee oh)* Latin origin. Derived from *aurum* (gold). It also has its roots in the old Roman family name of Aurēlius. A few saints have borne this name.

Ausencio *(ow sehn' see oh)* Latin origin. The name means to grow. The name appears eight times in the *Dictionary of Saints*.

Austreberto *(ows tray bair' toe)* German origin. The name combines the elements *ostar* (east) and *beraht* (brilliance): hence the name means brilliance from the east. Since the sun rises in the east, the name can also be translated to mean dawn or daybreak. Male and female variations of this name appear in the *Dictionary of Saints*. Variation: Austruberto.

Auxilio *(owks ee' lee oh)* Latin origin. The name means aid or protection. Modifications of this name appears three times in the *Dictionary of Saints*. Variation: Auxibio.

Bacilio *(bah see' lee oh)* Greek origin. The name means king or majesty. Of the several saints bestowed with this name, the best known was St. Basil the Great, who was famous for his great scholarly work. Diminutives: Bacho, Chilo. Variations: Basibo, Basil, Bastilla.

Baldomero *(ball doe may' ro)* German origin. The name derives from the German Waldemar, which gets its roots from combining the elements *wald* (powerful ruler) and *mari* (famous): hence the arrangement means infamous or legendary for his leadership. Diminutives: Balde, Valdo. Variations: Baldemas, Valdino, Waldemar.

Baltasar *(ball' ta sahr)* Semetic origin. The name means God protects your life. The name was borne by one of the Three Wise Men who visited the holy family and brought gifts to Christ after his birth.

Baptisto *(bap tee' stow)* Greek origin. The name is derived from *baptista* (a Baptist or one who baptizes). When a child is christened with this name it is usually in honor of John the Baptist. It is believed John's work prepared the people to accept Jesus Christ's teachings. Variation: Bautista.

Bardomiano *(bar doe mee ahn' no)* Latin origin. The name means son by adoption. The martyr by this name is honored with a feast day on September 25.

Barnabus *(bar' nah bus)* Hebrew origin. The name means son of consolation. In Latin and Greek the name is known as a plea or sermon. Although St. Barnabus was not considered one of the Twelve he is still remembered as an apostle or one who is sent. He worked ceaselessly to bring Christianity to the people of the Roman Empire. He later became a disciple of Paul. His connection with harvesters is due to the fact that his feast day falls on the old Midsummer Day. Variation: Bernabé.

Bartolomé *(bar toe low may')* Hebrew origin. The name has several meanings, including son of Tolmai or son of a farmer. In another sense of the word, the name translates to one who can thrive in the furrows. In addition to other saints bestowed with this given name, St. Bartolomé was one of the original twelve disciples. Diminutives: Barto, Tola. Variation: Bartelomeo.

Baudilio *(bough dee' lee oh)* Celtic origin. The name means victory. There are approximately four hundred churches in France dedicated to St. Baudilio, who helped spread Christianity in the third and fourth centuries. Diminutive: Lilo. Variation: Baudilion.

Belisario *(bay lee sah' ree oh)* Greek origin. The name means arrow or bowman. Belisario Domínguez was a leading force in the Mexican Revolution. Diminutive: Chayo. Variation: Bilisario.

Benedicto *(bay nay deek' toe)* Latin origin. The name means blessed. Although many saints were bestowed with this name, the one revered the most is St. Benedicto, father of the Holy Rule, also known as the Benedictine Rule. He was a great healer and well-known, respected teacher. His widespread influence is still felt in the West today. His esteemed teaching order focuses on the tradition of learning, the arts, and hospitality. Diminutives: Beni, Bento. Variations: Bendito, Benedetto, Benito.

Benigno *(bay neeg' no)* Latin origin. The name means beneficent (reaping the rewards from kindness and acts of charity) or merely the quality of being kind and generous. Variations: Benegno, Venino.

Benito *(bay nee' toe)* Latin origin. The name means to admire another or to speak well or kindly of someone. Diminutive: Nito. Variations: Benentio, Benitario.

Benjamín *(behn hah meen')* Hebrew origin. The name means son of my right hand or favorite son. In the Bible, he was the youngest son of Jacob and Rachel. It is also believed that he was Jacob's favorite son. He founded one tribe. In addition, many saints bore this name. Diminutives: Benja, Chemin, Mincho. Variations: Benjamé, Benjamo.

Berilo *(bay ree' low)* Greek origin. A Spanish derivative of the Greek *bēyllos* (sea-green gem). Beryl crystallizes in prismatic crystals such as aquamarine. Aquamarine is known as the stone of courage. Variation: Barilio.

Bernardo *(bare nar' doe)* German origin. The name combines the elements *bern* (bear) and *hard* (hearty, strong, powerful): hence the name means strong as a bear. St. Bernardo of Montjoux's life work consisted of ministering to travelers and inhabitants of the Alps. His position as the patron saint of skiers and mountaineers is a reflection of his pastoral care of the people. The large, longhaired mountain rescue dogs were named after him. The more ecclesiastically honored St. Bernardo of Clairvaux successfully played a major role in politics and church council. He wrote so eloquently that he became known as "Doctor Mellifluous" or "the honey-sweet doctor." This is also the origin of his patronage of beekeepers, honey, and candle makers. Hence the saying "You get more bees with honey than vinegar." Diminutives: Nino, Tato. Variations: Bernal, Bernadino, Venardo.

Bertrán *(bare trahn')* German origin. The name means bright raven. The raven symbolizes magic and knowledge of what the Native American people call the Great Mystery. The raven is believed to carry the energy of ceremonial magic from the ritual or prayer circle to the intended person. This name appears several times in the *Dictionary of Saints*.

Bienvenido *(bain bay nee' doe)* Italian origin. The name means welcome. Several saints had this given name.

Blasio *(blah' see oh)* Latin origin. The name means stuttering. In the fourth century, St. Blasio fled persecution by hiding out in a cave. From this station he ministered sick and wounded animals—which became the basis of his patronage of wild animals. Variations: Blas, Blasido.

Bonaventura *(bo nah bane toor' ah)* Latin origin. The name combines the Italian elements *bona* (good, fair) and *ventura* (luck, fortune): hence the name means good fortune. In another sense of the name it can be translated with the arrangement of the Latin *bonus* (good) with *ventus* (wind): in this way the name is good wind, which of course if you are a sailor the meanings are synonymous. Therefore it is no wonder that one of the California Spanish missions established on a Pacific coast seaport was named after San Buenaventura on March 31, 1782. The name appears seven times in the *Dictionary of Saints* as well. Diminutive: Ventura. Variations: Bonovento, Buenaventura.

Bonifacio *(bo nee fah' see oh)* Latin origin. The name combines the elements *bonum* (good) and *fatum* (fate): hence the name means fortunate or destined for good fate. Of the several saints bearing this name the saint most remembered helped to convert pagans living in Germany. Diminutives: Boni, Chacha, Facha. Variations: Bonaciano, Bonifasio.

Calvino *(call bee' no)* Latin origin. Derived from the Latin *calvinus* (bald). French Protestant Jean Calvin founded the Calvinist doctrines in the sixteenth century.

Camilo *(cah mee' low)* Latin origin. The name means child of free and noble birth. A saint by this name founded the Camellians Order of the Fathers of Good Death. Diminutive: Camito. Variations: Camillo, Camireno.

Candelario *(cahn day lah' ree oh)* Latin origin. Derived from the Spanish *candelario* (wax candle). The name refers to the Catholic feast day known as La Purificación de Nuestra Señora (the Purification of the Virgin Mother) held on February 2. Many candles are lit as a symbol of illuminating the path in the middle of winter for the holy family on their visit to the temple. Diminutive: Candedo. Variation: Candelano.

Candido *(cahn dee' doe)* Latin origin. The name means glowing white. The name appears sixteen times in the *Dictionary of Saints*.

Carlos *(car' lohs)* German origin. The name comes from the German *karl* (strong or manly). St. Carlos spent his personal money and all his energy caring for the sick at the time of the plague. He also founded Sunday schools for the Confraternity of Christian Doctrine. Diminutives: Carlito, Los.

Cayetano *(kye yea tah' no)* Latin origin. Derived from the town of Caieta. This fifteenth-century saint was a renowned scholar and a commanding force in the Counter-Reformation. Diminutive: Tano. Variations: Caitano, Cayitan, Cojetano.

Cecilio *(say see' lee oh)* Latin origin. Derived from the old Roman surname of Caecilius, which has its roots in *caecus* (blind, dim-sighted). Several saints bore this name, including a fasting companion of St. Cyprian. Diminutive: Celio. Variation: Sicilio.

Ceferino *(say fay ree' no)* Latin origin. The name means gentle breeze. It also connotes the personification of the West Wind, known as Zephyr from Greek folklore. Pope Zephyrin from the third century is remembered for his stout determination in defending Christ's divinity. Diminutives: Ceffo, Sef. Variations: Cefenro, Sepherino, Zephrin.

Celedonio *(say lay doe' nee oh)* Greek origin. The name refers to the swallow, a bird with dependable migratory patterns. The swallow's return to Mission San Juan Capistrano is so consistent that an annual celebration is planned every year to witness their magnificent return to their summer home. Variations: Celedón, Selidonio.

Celestino *(say lay stee' no)* Latin origin. Derived from the Roman family name of Caelius, which has its roots in *caelum* (heaven): hence the name has come to mean belonging to heaven. Variations: Celio, Selistino.

César *(say' sahr)* Latin origin. Derived from *caesaries* (having adundant hair). Diminutive: Chayo. Variations: Cesario, Sezario.

Cipriano *(see pree ah' no)* Latin origin. The name means one who comes from Cyprus. The saint by this name was the bishop of Carthage in the third century. He was quite instrumental in the development of Christian thought. Diminutives: Sipio, Yano. Variations: Cipreano, Cypriano.

Ciríaco *(see ree' ah co)* Greek origin. The name means belonging to the Lord. Variations of this name appear twelve times in the *Dictionary of Saints*. Diminutive: Yaco. Variations: Cirido, Quirico.

Cirilo *(see ree' lo)* Greek origin. Derived from the Greek *kyrios* (lordly). In the Persian language it means sun. The Persian king of Cyrus the Great ruled a vast empire in sixth century B.C. Many saints bore this name. Diminutive: Ciro. Variation: Cyrus.

Claudio *(klau' dee oh)* Latin origin. The name is derived from the Roman surname of Claudius, which has its roots in *claudus* (lame). The name is mentioned in the *Dictionary of Saints* over forty times. Diminutive: Cloyo. Variation: Claudicio.

Cleandro *(clay ahn' dro)* Greek origin. This name combines the elements *kloe* (glory, triumphant) and *andros* (man): hence the meaning is a triumphant man or man of glory. Variation: Cleanto.

Clemente *(clay men' tay)* Latin origin. The name means mild, lenient, or merciful. Of the many saints bestowed with this name the best known was St. Clemente, the fourth pope. He received martyrdom when he was tied to an anchor and thrown into the sea. It is believed that angels created his tomb, which is rumored to be visible only once a year at particularly low tides. Therefore, towns named after this saint are usually found on the coast. Diminutives: Mencha, Tente. Variations: Clementio, Clemte.

Cleto *(clay' toe)* Greek origin. The name means illustrious. A man bearing this name became the second successor of St. Peter. Variation: Cleyto.

Conrado *(cone rah' doe)* German origin. The name combines the old German elements *kuon* (bold, wise) and *rat* (counsel): hence the name means wise counsel. Eleven saints with this name are honored. Variation: Conrodo.

Constancio *(cone stawn' see oh)* Latin origin. The name means constancy. Variations of this name appear in the *Dictionary of Saints* forty-one times. The fourth-century ruler Constantine the Great converted to Christianity and played a major role in spreading his faith among the people. Diminutives: Conso, Stanzo. Variations: Constantine, Constanz.

Cornelio *(core nay' lee oh)* Latin origin. The name means long life; it's also a Greek derivation of the cornel tree, which was sacred to Apollo. Dogwood or bunchberry shrubs are from the cornel family and are deciduous. In other words they fertilize themselves, renewing and growing stronger with each year. In addition they don't succumb to diseases, making them hearty, long-lasting trees. This name could also be derived from *cornu* (horn), possibly like the one-horned unicorn, the immortal animal. In this way the three definitions connote some form of long life. Nineteen saints bore this name. Diminutives: Melio, Nelo. Variations: Cornello, Cornilio.

Cosme *(coze' may)* Greek origin. The name means order, refering to the harmony or consistency of the cosmos, universe. Cosme and Damián were third-century twin physicians in Cilicia who would accept no money for their services. Variation: Cosmas.

Crespín *(crays peen')* Latin origin. The name means curly hair. Although there are eighteen saints with this name, the first was a shoemaker who diligently made shoes for the poor, hence his patronage of shoemakers. Diminutives: Cres, Pino. Variation: Crispin.

Crisanto *(kree sahn' toe)* Greek origin. Derived from the Greek *chrysanthemon* (golden flower). Variations of the chrysanthemum flower can be edible while others are used for medicinal purposes. Several saints bore this name. Variations: Cresanto, Crizanto.

Crisóforo *(kree so' for ro)* Greek origin. The name is
a combination of Christos (Christ) and *pherein* (to
bear): hence the name means Christ bearer. St. Crisóforo was a giant of a man known originally as Offero.
He lived with a hermit who ferried people across a
wide river. One stormy night a young child begged for
passage across the raging river. As he trod through the
wild water the giant found the weight of the small child
to be nearly unbearable. Staff in hand, he struggled
desperately to reach the other bank. When they arrived
safely the child revealed himself as Jesus Christ and
told Offero that his name would now be Crisóforo,
meaning Christ bearer. It is said that the burden Crisóforo carried across that turbulent river was the
weight of the whole world. Many modern-day surfers
wear a pendant of St. Crisóforo carrying the Christ
upon his shoulders for protection against tempestuous
waves of the ocean.

Cristián *(krees tee ahn')* Greek origin. Derived from
the Greek *christiānus* (belonging to the religion of Jesus Christ or a follower of Christ). Spanish cognate of
Christian.

Cristo *(krees' toe)* Greek origin. Derived from the Greek
christos (the anointed), which has its roots in *chrien*
(to anoint). Another sense of the word translates to
useful or of service. Variation: Cristelo.

Cristóbal *(krees toe' vahl)* Greek origin. The name
means Christ bearer.

Cruz *(kruce)* Latin origin. Derived from the Spanish *cruz*
(cross or crucifix). Refers to the cross upon which
Christ was killed.

Cuauhtémoc *(cwao tay' moke)* Aztec origin. The name
means eagle that falls. The eagle represents our connection to the divine. It symbolizes the refinement one
achieves through facing life's challenges by trust-

ing in one's abilities and bonding with God, the source of all our good. The feathers of the eagle are considered to be the most sacred of all. Another name for the Aztec language is Nahuatl. The use of Indian names is recently on the rise. The advanced Aztecs have been the primary source for the indigenous names.

Curcio *(koor' see oh)* French origin. The name means courteous.

Dámaso *(dah' mah so)* Greek origin. Derived from the Greek *damān* (to tame). A fourth-century pope and doctor bore this name. Variations: Damacio, Damasiano, Dómaso.

Damián *(dah mee ahn')* Greek origin. Derived from the Greek *damān* (to tame) hence the name means tamer or guide. St. Damián is usually associated with his twin brother, St. Cosmas. The brothers worked together administering their medicinal services without pay. Variation: Damiano.

Daniel *(dahn yell')* Hebrew origin. Derived from *dāni'ēl* (God judges or the Lord is my judge). Daniel was a biblical prophet who is most remembered for his escape from the lion's den. The name appears thirty-five times in the *Dictionary of Saints*. Diminutives: Nelo, Nilo. Variations: Danilo, Donelo.

Dante *(don' tay)* Italian origin. The name means to endure.

Darío *(dahr ree' oh)* Greek origin. The name means he who upholds the good or wealthy.

David *(dah beed')* Hebrew origin. Derived from *dāvīd* (beloved). In another sense of the word the name means friend: hence one can translate the name to mean beloved friend. In the Bible, one of the most famous people bestowed with this name was a mere shepherd who fought the giant Goliath with a slingshot.

He later became the king of Israel and presumed author of many psalms. Variation: Dabid.

Delgadino *(dell gah dee' no)* Spanish origin. Derived from the Spanish surname Delgado (slender, delicate, or smooth and fine).

Delmar *(del mahr)* Latin origin. The name derives from the elements *del* (of) and *mar* (sea): hence the name means of the sea or mariner.

Demetrio *(day may' tree oh)* Greek origin. The name means belonging to Demeter, the Greek goddess of agriculture and fertility. She oversees the development of all growing things, but in particular is the guardian of grain. The name appears fifty-three times in the *Dictionary of Saints.* Diminutive: Mecho. Variations: Demeterio, Demstrio.

Democles *(day mo' clays)* Greek origin. Derived from the Greek Damoklēs (glory of the people). The name has its roots in a combination of the elements *dēmos* (people, population) and *kleos* (glory). An ambitious Syracusan courtier by this name attended a banquet where a sword was suspended above his head. This act was intended to be a lesson to teach him the perils of being a king and it is from this parable that the expression "the sword of Damocles" originated. Variation: Damocles.

Deogracias *(day oh grah' see ahs)* Latin origin. The name combines the elements *deo* (God) and *gracias* (thanks): hence the name means thanks to God. A fifth-century bishop ministered prisoners after the sack of Rome. Variation: Diogracias.

Desiderio *(day see day' ree oh)* Latin origin. From the Latin word *desiderium* (desiring, yearning, or grief for an absent person). Variant cognates of this name appear eleven times in the *Dictionary of Saints.* Diminutives: Desi, Yeyo. Variations: Dejiderio, Desidereo, Desuderio.

Diego *(dee ā go)* Latin origin. Derived from the Hebrew *ya'aqob* (seizing by the heel or supplanting). Often bestowed as an independent given name, the name is a diminutive of Jaime, which is a Spanish cognate of James. James evolved from the Latin Iacobus, which has its roots in the Greek Iakōbos, a name that originates from the Hebrew Yaakov. Mission San Diego was the first mission established by Father Serra and his party.

Dimas *(dee mahs)* Slavic origin. The name means strong fighter.

Diomedes *(dee oh may' days)* Greek origin. The name means thought or plan.

Dionisio *(dee o nee' see oh)* Greek origin. The name means sacred to Dionysus. Dionysus was the Greek god of fertility, wine, and revelry. Variations of this name appear sixty-eight times in the *Dictionary of Saints*. Diminutive: Nicho. Variations: Deniso, Dyonisio.

Domingo *(doe meen' go)* Latin origin. Derived from *dominus* (a lord or master): hence the name means of the Lord. It also refers to Sunday and is bestowed to children born on this day. Of the several saints bearing this name the most revered was St. Domingo, a Spaniard whose religious zest arose from his fight against heresy. While pregnant with him, Domingo's mother had a vision of her son as a dog holding a flaming torch; thus the nickname for the Dominican Order is "the hounds of God." Diminutive: Mingo. Variations: Dominciano, Domino.

Donaciano *(doe nah see ah' no)* Spanish origin. Derived from the Latin *donare* (to give or donate). In modern translation the name has come to mean a gift or donation. Of the seventy-five saints who bore this name the most honored was a fourth-century bishop of Casae Nigrae. He held rigorous views concerning purity and wholesomeness and founded a North African Christian sect. Diminutive: Chano. Variations: Donacio, Donato, Donotiano.

Donaldo *(doe nahl' doe)* Gaelic origin. Derives from Domhnall (world ruler). In a similar sense the name means prince of the universe. Variation: Donaldonio.

Dositeo *(doe' see tay' oh)* Greek origin. The name means gift of God.

Edgardo *(ayd gahr' doe)* Anglo-Saxon origin. The name means spear or javelin. Diminutive: Lalo. Variations: Edgar, Edgrado.

Edmundo *(aid moon' doe)* Anglo-Saxon origin. This is a combination of the elements *ēad* (wealth, rich, prosperous) and *mund* (hand or protection): hence the name means wealthy protection or protection of prosperity. There were a few saints with this name. Diminutive: Mundo.

Eduardo *(ā dwahr doe)* Anglo-Saxon origin. This name combines the elements *ēad* (wealth, rich, prosperous) and *weard* (guardian or protector): hence the name means rich guardian. Diminutives: Duardo, Guayo. Variations: Eduarelo, Edward.

Eferino *(aay fay ree' no)* Latin origin. Derived from the Latin *efferus* (fierce).

Efraín *(ā frah een')* Hebrew origin. Derived from *ephrayim* (very fruitful). In the Bible he was the younger son of Joseph and founded the tribe of Ephraim. Many saints bore this name. Diminutive: Juncho. Variations: Efaím, Efrin, Ephrain.

Eleázar *(ā lee ah' zar)* Hebrew origin. Spanish form of Lazarus, which has its roots in *el'āzār* (God has

helped). Variations of the name are found throughout
the Bible. Aaron's third son who became the high
priest after his father, as well as Abraham's steward
and Moses' son all bore this name. Nine saints bore
this name. Variations: Eleásar, Elicerio, Eliezer.

Eleuterio *(aay lay oo tay' ree oh)* Greek origin. Derived from *eleutheria* (liberty, freedom). Over twenty
saints appear with this name in the *Dictionary of
Saints*. Diminutives: Teyo, Xlut. Variations: Elentoriz,
Elouterio.

Elián *(eh lee ahn')* Spanish origin. This is a combination
of Elizabeth (God is my oath) and Juan (God is gracious): hence the name means he who is assured, compassionate grace, or mercy.

Elías *(ā lee' ahs)* Hebrew origin. Spanish cognate of
Elijah, which is derived from *ēlīyāhū* (Jehovah is God).
Diminutive: Lincha. Variation: Eliaz.

Eligio *(aay lee' hee oh)* Latin origin. The name means
the elect. Of the three saints that bore this name the
most revered is a seventh-century minter and gold-
smith. Variations: Elijo, Eloi, Eloy.

Eliseo *(ā lee say' oh)* Hebrew origin. Spanish cognate
of Elisha, which is derived from *elīshā* (God is my
health and salvation). The name appears nine times in
the *Dictionary of Saints*. Diminutives: Cheyo, Licha.
Variations: Eliseo, Elysiuio.

Eloiso *(aay low ee' so)* German origin. The name means
complete. Diminutive: Lucha. Variations: Elocio, Elo-
sio.

Elpidio *(ehl pee' dee oh)* Greek origin. The name means
hope. At least fifteen saints bore this name. Variation:
Elpodio.

Emilio *(ā mee' lee oh)* German and Latin origin. It may
be derived from the German *amal* (work): hence the

name has come to mean industrious. While others believe the name has its roots in the Latin surname Aemilius, which comes from *aemulus* (to emulate or imitate in an effort to equal or excel).

Enrique *(enn ree' kay)* German origin. The name is the Spanish equivalent to the German Heinrich (ruler of a residence or home ruler). Another source states that the name means king of the forest. Sixteen saints were bestowed with this name. Diminutives: Kiko, Erik, Quinto. Variations: Enriques, Henrico.

Epifanio *(ā pee fah' nee oh)* Greek origin. Derived from *epiphaneia* (appearance, manifestation). The name relates to the Epiphany, which honors three events: the visit of the Three Wise Men, or Magi; the baptism of Jesus; and Jesus' first miracle at Cana. Diminutive: Pifano. Variations: Epifonio, Espín.

Erasmo *(ā rahs' mo)* Greek origin. Derived from Erasmios (lovely), which has its roots in *eran* (to love): hence the name has come to mean worthy of love or lovely. Variations: Elmo, Erasumus.

Erasto *(ā rahs' toe)* Greek origin. Derived from Erastos (beloved), which has its roots in *eran* (to love): hence the name has come to mean worthy of love or beloved. Variation: Erastro.

Erico *(ā oo ree' ko)* German origin. The name combines the elements of *ehre* (honor, admiration) and *rīk* (ruler, king): hence the name means admirable king. In another sense, the name gets its roots from the Old Norse Eirikr, which derives from *ei* (everlasting, eternity) and *rikr* (ruler, king): hence the name is eternal ruler. Variation: Eurique.

Ernesto *(air nay' sto)* German origin. The name means earnest, steadfast, and sincere. Diminutives: Ernio, Nesto. Variations: Ernestor, Ernilo.

Esau *(aay say ooh')* Hebrew origin. The name means covered with hair. In the Bible, he was the son of Rebekah and Isaac. He sold his birthright to his brother Jacob.

Estanislao *(ā stahn' ees lah oh)* Slavic origin. A combination of *stan* (government) and *slav* (glorious): hence the name means glorious government. Diminutives: Lalo, Tani. Variations: Estamislao, Estansilio.

Esteban *(ā stay' bahn)* Greek origin. Derived from the Latin Stephanus, which has its roots in the Greek Steaphanos (a crown, wreath that adorns the head). Although there are eighty-two saints bestowed with this name, the one most honored was St. Esteban, the first Christian martyr and powerful preacher. He was a safeguard, chosen by the community to become one of the seven deacons (assistants to the disciples), and some believe he was their head. He demonstrated great wonders and experienced visions. Diminutive: Fani. Variations: Estavén, Estefino, Stephano.

Estuardo *(ā stoo are' doe)* Spanish cognate of the English Stuart (steward or park ranger).

Eugenio *(ā oo hay' nee oh)* Greek origin. Derived from *eugenēs* (well-born, aristocratic). The name appears fifty-four times in the *Dictionary of Saints*. Diminutive: Geño. Variations: Eginito, Eugercio.

Eulogio *(ā oo low' hee oh)* Greek origin. The name combines the elements of *eu* (good, fine, well) with *logikos* (reasoning, speaking): hence the name means he who is a good orator. Possibly in an effort to effectively spread the word of Christianity thirteen saints bore this name. Diminutive: Locho. Variations: Eluochio, Olijio.

Eusebio *(ā oo say' bee oh)* Greek origin. The name combines the elements *eu* (good, fine, well) and *sebein* (to worship or pray): hence the arrangement means the pious one or religious one.

Eustacio *(aay ooh stah' see oh)* Greek origin. Spanish cognate of Eustace, which derives from *eustachys,* a combination of the elements *eu* (well) and *stachys* (ear of grain, as in corn): hence the name means rich in corn or fruitful, abundant. In another translation the name means firm, consistent, or constant. Hopefully if you were a farmer your crops of corn would be consistently abundant, so we can see a possible connection between the two meanings. Variation: Euschio.

Evaristo *(ā bah ree' sto)* Greek origin. The name means well or good, taking its meaning from the element *eu* (good). In addition to four saints bearing this name, the fourth pope also bore this name. It is he who divided ancient Rome into parishes and deaconries. Variation: Ebaristo.

Everardo *(ā bay rahr' doe)* German origin. The name combines the elements *ebur* (wild boar) and *harto* (strong): hence the name means strong as a boar. The wild boar was another animal sacred to the Native American people. The boar represents the courage needed to confront the greatest challenges in life, whether that is changing a weakness within into a strength, or facing a difficult relationship or any turning point within our lives, but most importantly accepting the whole truth about the people and situations in our lives. Boar medicine implores us to meet the problem head-on in an active, determined manner that will allow us to reclaim our spirit's energy. A few saints bore this name. Diminutive: Lalo. Variations: Averando, Eberardo, Everaldo.

Ezequías *(ā zay kee' ahs)* Hebrew origin. Derived from *hizqīyāh* (God will strengthen). In the Bible, he was a king of Judah and known for his ability to gov-

ern well. He reigned in the time of Isaiah. Diminutive:
Checo. Variations: Esequiz, Ezequís.

Ezequiel *(ā zay kee ell')* Hebrew origin. Derived from
yehezq'ēl (God will strengthen). In the Bible, a prophet
by this name known as a great visionary could describe
the future with great detail and color. His prophecies
are recorded in the Old Testament book of Ezekiel.
Diminutives: Chequelo, Quiel, Ziek. Variations: Ese-
quiel, Ezekiel.

Fabián *(fah bee ahn')* Latin origin. Derived from the
Roman surname Fabius, which has its roots in *faba* (a
bean). The name appears sixteen times in the
Dictionary of Saints. Variation: Fabio.

Faustino *(fouse tee' no)* Latin origin. Derived from
Faustus (bringer of good luck), which has its roots in
fauste (prosperous, lucky, fortunate). The name appears
eighty-seven times in the *Dictionary of Saints.* Diminutive: Faz. Variation: Faustano.

Febronio *(fay broe' nee oh)* Latin origin. Derived from
the month of February. Also relates to the feast of La
Purificación de Nuestra Señora held on February 2.
Variation: Frebrico.

Federico *(fay day ree ko)* German origin. Derived from
Friedrich, which combines the elements *frithu* (peace)
and *rīk* (ruler): hence the name means ruler of peace.
The name also relates simply to the qualities of power
and peace. Diminutive: Lico. Variation: Fredico.

Felipo *(fay lee' po)* Greek origin. Combines the elements *philos* (loving) and *hippos* (horses): hence the
name means lover of horses. Of the fifty-five saints
bestowed with this name the most important is Philip
the Apostle. Diminutive: Felo. Variations: Felipe,
Philip.

Félix *(fay' leeks)* Latin origin. The name means merry or lucky. St. Felix escaped persecution with the help of an angel. He hid in a cave, whereupon a spider immediately spun an elaborate web that covered the entrance of the cave, concealing the hidden man. He was known for his compassion and generosity. Diminutives: Chito, Felichi. Variations: Felecidad, Feliciano, Felicismo.

Fernando *(fare nahn' doe)* German origin. This name has many translations. It is derived from these possible elements: *frithu* (peace), *fardi* (voyage), or *ferchivus* (childlike spirit) and *nanths* (bravery), *nand* (prepared, ready), or *nanthi* (daring, risk). From these components various arrangements can be made including the adventurous yet composed risk taker, or the wanderlust-struck courageous traveler, or he who makes peace on a dangerous trek. Diminutive: Nando. Variation: Fernedo.

Fidel *(fee dell')* Latin origin. Derived from *fidelis* (faithful, loyal, trustworthy). In the Victorian period, wedding portraits were commissioned with dogs in the picture because they represented loyalty: hence the pet name Fido for dogs became popular. Diminutive: Fido. Variation: Fidelio.

Fidencio *(fee dayn' see oh)* Latin origin. The name means confidence or self-assurance. Several saints bore this name. Variation: Fidensio.

Filadelfo *(fee lah del' fo)* Latin origin. Derived from Philadelphus, the name means brotherly love.

Filemón *(fee lay moan')* Greek origin. The name means loving or affectionate. According to Greek mythology, Philemon and Baucis were the only ones who offered shelter to Zeus and Hera. Afterward they received eternal life, being immortalized as trees. Variations: Felemon, Philemon.

Filiberto *(fee lee bare' toe)* German origin. A combination of *fila* (much) with *beraht* (bright, famous, celebrated): hence the name means exceptionally celebrated or well known. Variation: Fileberto.

Florencio *(flor ren' see oh)* Latin origin. Derived from *florens* (blooming, abundant, burgeoning). The name appears sixty-six times in the *Dictionary of Saints.* Diminutives: Poncho, Tino. Variation: Florenzo.

Fortunato *(fore too nah' toe)* Latin origin. Derived from *fortūnātus* (fortunate, lucky). Variations of this name are found sixty-nine times in the *Dictionary of Saints.* Variations: Fortunado, Furtanato.

Fortuno *(for too no)* Latin origin. Derived from *fortuna* (chance, fortune, fate). A goddess by this name was the deity in charge of luck and chance. Alternately she bestowed poverty and misfortune or riches and good luck. Diminutive: Tuno. Variation: Fortunio.

Francisco *(frahn sees' ko)* Latin origin. Derived from the French *franc* (free). The name also means from France or a freeman. Although there are forty-eight saints bestowed with this name, the most revered and beloved was St. Francis de Asís. He was the first to experience the stigmata—the five wounds of Christ from the cross. He is also remembered for his famous sermon to the birds and the inauguration of the Christmas crib. Diminutives: Paco, Pancho, Paquito. Variations: Francis, Franco.

Fructuoso *(frook too oh' so)* Latin origin. The name means fruitful, fertile, and abundant. Several saints bore this name, including a third-century bishop of Tarragona. Variations: Fructo, Frutoro.

Gabriel *(gah bree ell')* Hebrew origin. Derived from *gavhrī'ēl* (God is strong or God is my strength). Gabriel had the honor of being the archangel and messenger of God. He announced God's plan to save the world to Mary with the proclamation, "Thou shalt conceive in thy womb, and bring forth a son, and shall call his name Jesus." Diminutive: Gabe. Variations: Abrielo, Gabril.

Galeno *(gah lay' no)* Greek origin. Derived from *galēnē* (calm). An alternate meaning is little bright one.

García *(gahr see' ah)* Spanish origin. Borrowed from the Spanish surname, meaning fox. Fox represents the ability to melt into one's surroundings in order to observe unnoticed. His art is that of camouflage, akin to a chameleon. His best medicine, though, is as one who protects the well-being of the family unit. Another source indicates the name boasts Teutonic origins and means mighty with the spear.

Gaspar *(gahs par')* Persian origin. The name means master of treasure. Gaspar was one of the three Magi who brought gifts to the Christ child on the night of his birth. Gaspar de Portola led the calvary in charge of protecting Father Serra as they established the mission system in California during the late eighteenth and early nineteenth century. Variation: Gazpar.

Gastón *(gahs tone')* Teutonic origin. The name means hospitable.

Gedeón *(hay day own')* Hebrew origin. Derived from *gidh'ōn* (hewer, one who cuts down trees). From another source the name has the following translations: mighty warrior, a fighter, and a judge.

Gemino *(hay mee' no)* Latin origin. Derived from *gemini* (meaning twin, which refers to the twins Castor and Pollux). It is also the third sign of the zodiac and reigns from late May to late June. People born under this sign usually exhibit polar personality traits. Often they are perceptive, inquisitive, and persistent.

Génaro *(hay' nah ro)* Latin origin. Derived from Januarius (the month of Janus, or as we now know it, January). Janus was the Roman god of beginnings and endings. He had two faces that looked in opposite directions. The name appears sixty-two times in the *Dictionary of Saints.*

Generoso *(hehn ehr oh so)* Latin origin. The name means generous.

Geraldo *(hay rahl' doe, jer rahl' doe)* German origin. The name is a combination of *ger* (spear) and *wald* (rule, lead): hence the name means spear ruler or to lead with a spear. Eight saints carried this name. Variation: Giralda.

Gerardo *(hay rahr' doe, jer rahr' Doe)* German origin. The name is a combination of *ger* (spear) and *hart* (hearty, forceful, strong): hence the name means forceful or strong with a spear. Sixteen saints were bestowed with this name. Variation: Gernado.

Germán *(hair mahn')* German origin. This name is a combination of the elements *hari* (army) or *ger* (spear) and *man* (man): hence the name means either soldier or man with a spear.

Gervasio *(hare bah' see oh)* Teutonic origin. Combination of the German elements *ger* (spear) with the Celtic *vass* (servant): hence the name means servant of the spear. Variations: Gervacio, Jervaso.

Gilberto *(heel bare' toe)* German origin. The arrangement is composed of *gisil* (pledge) and *beraht* (bright, renowned): hence the name means renowned pledge. Diminutives: Beto, Gil. Variations: Gilberso, Hilberto.

Gonzalo *(gone zah' low)* German origin. The name means a fight or combat. There are five saints bestowed with this name. Diminutive: Gonzi. Variation: Gonzales.

Gregorio *(gray go' ree oh)* Greek origin. The name comes from the Greek Grēgorios (watchman), which has its roots in *egeirein* (to awaken). There have been many Gregarios canonized in the Roman martyrdom, but the most revered are Gregario the Great and Gregario the Wondermaker. One year after becoming the civil magistrate of Rome, Gregario the Great decided to dedicate his life to Christ. He sold much of his wealth and became a monk, and ten years later, he was elected pope. He wrote the *Pastoral Care,* explaining and reorganizing the office and duties of bishops, which became a key text for the medieval church. Today he is remembered for his work with church singers: the Gregorian chant is named after him. Gregario the Wondermaker earned his title from the many miracles he performed, including several that manipulated the elements, such as redirecting a river, moving a mountain, and invoking an earthquake.

Guido *(ghee doe)* Teutonic origin. The name means famous guide.

Guillermo *(ghee yare' mo)* German origin. Compounding of the elements *willeo* (will, resolution) and *helm* (helmet, protection): hence the name means helmet of resolution or protector with a strong will. The name appears fifty times in the *Dictionary of Saints.* Diminutives: Guico, Memo. Variations: Giermo, Guillelmo.

Gumersindo *(goo mare seen' doe)* German origin. The name means road of war. Diminutive: Chindo. Variation: Guimenindo.

Gustavo *(go stah' bo)* Teutonic origin. The name means holding the staff of royalty or even the staff of the gods. Diminutives: Chavo, Tavito. Variations: Gustabo, Gutavo.

Héctor *(eck' tore)* Greek origin. Derived from Hecktōr (holding fast), which has its roots in *echein* (to hold or to have): the name now means steadfast or unwavering. Diminutives: Eto, Tito. Variations: Ector, Hecktor.

Helio *(ay' lee oh)* Greek origin. The name means sun. Variation: Elio.

Heliodoro *(aay lee oh doe' roe)* Greek origin. The name is a compounding of *hēlios* (sun) and *dōron* (gift): hence the name means gift of the sun. The name is mentioned ten times in the *Dictionary of Saints*. Diminutive: Dor. Variation: Elidoro.

Heráclio *(air a' klee oh)* Greek origin. The name is a composition of Hēra (the queen of the Greek pantheon and wife of Zeus) and *kleos* (glory): hence the name means abiding in the glory or grandeur of Hera. In another sense of the word, since she was royalty of divinity the name also translates to divine glory. Variation: Heraclea.

Herberto *(air bare' toe)* Anglo-Saxon origin. A combination of the elements *here* (army) and *boerht* (bright, brilliant): hence the name means brilliant army. Diminutive: Heri. Variations: Ereberto, Heberto.

Herculano *(air koo lah' no)* Greek origin. This name means belonging to Hercules. This is a Spanish cognate of the Greek Hercules, a mythical Greek hero famous for his strength, size, and courage. It is also the namesake for a very large northern constellation. Several saints bore this name. Variations: Arculano, Herculese.

Hermán *(air mahn')* German origin. The name is an arrangement of *heri* (army) and *man* (man): hence the name means warrior or soldier. From another source the name means sacred place. Diminutive: Hermio. Variations: Arminio, Hermino.

Hermes *(her' mays)* Greek origin. The name means messenger. According to Greek mythology the god Hermes had three responsibilities: gods' messenger, delivering souls to Hades, and fertilizer of flocks. Eighteen saints were bestowed with this name. Variation: Hermenes.

Hesiquio *(aay see' key oh)* Hebrew origin. The name means strong in God. In the Bible he was the king of Judah for twenty-nine years. Over twenty saints bore this name. Diminutive: Chico. Variations: Ezekio, Ezquio.

Higinio *(ee hee' nee oh)* Greek origin. The name means healthy or he who has good health. According to Greek mythology, it is the personification of good health.

Hilario *(ee lah' ree oh)* Latin origin. Derived from *hilaris* (cheerful, happy, funny), which is the source for the word *hilarious*. The name appears thirty-five times in the *Dictionary of Saints*. Diminutive: Lalo. Variation: Helarió.

Homero *(oh may' ro)* Greek origin. Derived from *homēros* (blind). The renowned author of the *Iliad* and the *Odyssey* was bestowed with this name.

Horatio *(o rah' see oh)* Latin origin. Derived from the Roman surname of Horatius, which has its roots in *hora* (hour, time). Diminutive: Lacho. Variations: Horacio, Oracio.

Hugo *(ooh' go)* French origin. Derived from *hugu* (heart, mind). The name means he who has spiritual understanding and intelligence. St. Hugo, patron saint of swans, became associated with the bird when he tamed a wild swan and kept him as a pet. The swan would bury his head in Hugo's wide sleeve and follow him about the manor, returning to the wild when the saint was away from home.

Ignacio *(eeg nah' see oh)* Latin origin. Derived from the Roman surname of Egnatius, which has its roots in *ignis* (fire): hence the name has come to mean flaming, passionate. Of the several saints with this name the most revered is St. Ignatius of Loyola. He was a Spanish priest and founded the Society of Jesus, also known as the Jesuits. Diminutives: Nachito, Nacho. Variations: Igacio, Ignatius.

Indalecio *(een dah lay see oh)* Greek origin. Derived from Indaletios (of or like a teacher). He was a bishop of Spain who can now be invoked against drought. Variations: Eudalesio, Indelesio.

Inocencio *(ee no sane' see oh)* Latin origin. Derived from *innocens* (innocent). The name refers to the killing of all male children by order of Herod in his pursuit to kill the Christ child. Twenty-seven saints, including thirteen popes, bore this name. Variations: Innocención, Innocentio.

Isac *(ee sock')* Hebrew origin. Derived from *yitshāq* (laughter). Isaac is revered as one of the Hebrew patriarchs. In the Bible, he was the son of Abraham and Sarah. Later he became the father of Jacob. There were forty-eight saints with this name. Diminutive: Caco. Variation: Isaak.

Isaiah *(ee say' ah)* Hebrew origin. The name means God is salvation. Isaiah was a beloved prophet and is famous for his eloquent delivery and style in speaking.

Isandro *(ee sahn' dro)* Greek origin. Derived from Lysandros (freer of mankind, rescuer). The name is an arrangement of the elements *lysis* (freeing, releasing) and *man* (man).

Isidoro *(ee see dor' oh)* Greek origin. Derived from Isidoros (gift of Isis), which has its roots in the combination of Isis (revered Egyptian goddess of fertility and women) and *dōron* (gift). Although the name appears thirty-one times in the *Dictionary of Saints,* the most honored is an eleventh-century Spanish laborer. Diminutives: Cedro, Doro. Variations: Isadro, Izidero.

Ismael *(ees mah ell')* Hebrew origin. Derived from *yishmā'ē'l* (God hears). Ismael is the patriarch of the Arabs. Diminutive: Melito. Variations: Esmela, Ishmael.

Israel *(ees rah ell')* Hebrew origin. Derived from *yisrā'ēl* (wrestler with God). In the Bible, this name was confered upon Jacob after he wrestled with the archangel Michael. Diminutive: Isra. Variations: Isareal, Isreal.

Jacián *(hah see ahn')* Greek origin. Spanish equivalent to Jason. Derived from *iāson* (healer). According to the Greek pantheon he was the leader of the Argonauts who searched for the Golden Fleece.

Jacinto *(hah seen' toe)* Greek origin. The name means beautiful as a hyacinth.

Jaime *(hi' may)* Hebrew origin. The name means supplanter or to seize by the heel. Jaime is a Greek translation from the Hebrew Jacob. In the Bible, Jacob was the third patriarch and fathered twelve tribes. St. Jaime was one of the inner circle, the three closest to Jesus. Many of his followers journey to the cathedral in Santiago de Compostela, Spain. The badge for these pilgrims is the cockleshell and has since become one of the saint's symbols.

Jano *(hah' no)* Greek origin. The name means brilliant as the sun. Derived from the Greek god Janus, who is the guardian of the door of time and namesake for the month of January.

Javier *(hah bee air')* Derived from the Basque name Etcheberria (the new house). It is also believed that the name has its roots in the surname Xavier. St. Francis

Xavier was a sixteenth-century Spanish missionary who traveled to Japan and the East Indies. He is the patron saint who protects and guides missionaries in foreign lands.

Jeremías *(hay ray mee' ahs)* Hebrew origin. Derived from the Greek Hieremias, which comes from the Hebrew Yirmeyahau, a name that has its roots in *yirmeyāh* (God will raise up or the Lord will uplift). He was a great prophet but his ominous lectures angered many people. Eventually his gloomy approach aroused such resentment that he was put in jail for many years.

Jerónimo *(hay ro' nee mo)* Greek origin. Derived from Hieronymos (sacred name), which is a compounding of the elements *hieros* (holy or sacred) and *onyma* (name). St. Jerónimo is often depicted with a lion. He and the lion became compadres when the gentle Jerónimo extracted a thorn from the beast's paw. He is also known for his scholarly work. Instructed by Pope Damasus, Jerónimo translated the Greek and Hebrew books of the Bible into Latin. Variation: Gerónimo.

Jesús *(hay soos')* Hebrew origin. The name is a Greek equivalent of Joshua. Derived from the Latin Iesus, which comes from the Greek Iēsous, a name that has its roots in the Hebrew *yēshū'a*, a derivative of *yehōshū'a* (the Lord saves, God is salvation). The name is bestowed in honor of Jesus Christ, the founder of the Christian faith and religion, born to the Virgin María and St. Joseph. Parents hope to ensure the protection of the son of God when they bestow this name on their son. Diminutive: Chucho.

Joaquín *(hwa keen')* Hebrew origin. Derived from Jehoiakim, which is derived from Yehoyakim (God gives strength or God will establish). According to the Bible, Joaquin was the father of the Virgin María. Joaquin Murrietta, a Californio bandit in the 1850s, was regarded as a kind of Robin Hood. He stole from the rich and returned monies to the nineteenth-century Californios, during the madness of the goldrush and dispossession of the Latino landowners. Diminutives: Huacho, Quin. Variations: Joaquim, Joachín.

Jonás *(hoe nahs')* Hebrew origin. The name means gentle as a dove. He is remembered as the prophet who was swallowed by a whale. The name appears eighteen times in the *Dictionary of Saints.*

Jorge *(hor' hay)* Greek origin. Derived from *geōrges* (farmer, earthworker). St. Jorge was a fourth-century soldier remembered for his legendary chivalry. To rid their town of an evil dragon, the medieval people sent their princess to be sacrificed. Through his faith in Jesus Christ, Jorge killed the dragon by piercing him in the heart with his lance. The townspeople were so impressed that thousands were converted on that very day. Diminutive: Giorgio.

José *(ho say')* Hebrew origin. Popular cognate of Joseph. The name comes from the Greek Iōsēph, which is derived from the Hebrew Yosef, a name that has its roots in *yōsēf* (may God add or God will increase). St. José, a carpenter, was the earthly father of Jesus and responsible for taking care of the holy family. He is remembered as a just man, exhibiting the human qualities of being upright, meritorious, and true. His obedience and dedication to God's will is highly regarded. His feast day as the husband of Mary is March 19. May 1 is the feast day of José the worker. Diminutives: Pep, Pepito.

Josefat *(hoe say faht')* Hebrew origin. The name means he who has God as his judge.

Juan *(hwahn)* Hebrew origin. Derived from *yehōhānān* (Yahweh is gracious): hence the name has come to mean God is gracious or God has shown favor. Juan the Baptist was a cousin of Jesus and is remembered as the greatest of all prophets, who paved the way for Jesus' teachings. It is recorded that Jesus considered Juan to be the herald of the Messiah. It is also said that while in the womb Juan "leaped" for joy upon recognizing Jesus. The name appears 418 times in the *Dictionary of Saints.* Diminutive: Juanito.

Judas *(hoo' dahs)* Hebrew origin. The name means praise of God. In the Bible, he was the brother and apostle of Jesus, who betrayed the Christ in his last days, as well as the youngest son of Jacob and Leah, who founded one of the twelve tribes of Israel.

Julio *(hoo' lee oh)* Latin origin. The name means downy-bearded or youthful. Variation: Julián.

Junipero *(hoon ee peh' roe)* Anglo-Saxon origin. Believed to have derived from the juniper plant. Juniper has the qualities of being invigorating and revitalizing. The juniper berries are edible when properly prepared. Fray Junipero Serra founded the California mission system in the eighteenth century.

Justino *(hoos. tee' no)* Latin origin. Derived from Justinus, which has its roots in *justus* (just, upright, proper). Variation: Justano.

Ladislao *(lah dees lah' oh)* Slavic origin. Derived from Vladislav (glorious reign), which is composed of the elements *volod* (govern) and *slav* (glory). Diminutive: Lalo. Variation: Ladaslao.

Lauro *(la ooh' roe)* Latin origin. The name means laurel. Victors in various contests, especially the Olympics, were crowned with wreaths made of the foliage from the laurel tree. Diminutive: Laurino. Variation: Laureno.

Lázaro *(lah' zah ro)* Hebrew origin. Spanish equivalent of Lazarus, a form of the Greek Lazaros, which has its roots in *el'āzār* (God has given help). In the Bible, Lázaro was the brother of Martha and Mary. Jesus came to Bethany where Lázaro lay dead for four days, and told him to rise. Immediately Lázaro rose from his deathbed and was brought back to life.

Leandro *(lay ahn' dro)* Greek origin. Derived from the Greek Leander (lion man), a name that has its roots in the elements *leōn* (lion) and *andros* (man). Four saints were bestowed with this name, including a sixth-century bishop of Seville. Variation: Leodro.

León *(lay own')* Latin origin. Derived from *leo* (lion): hence the name means fearless as a lion. Leo is also the fifth sign of the zodiac. People born under this sign are often gregarious, dramatic, energetic, and prideful. Of the forty-eight saints who bore this name the most honored was a fifth-century pope, thought to be the second greatest of all popes.

Leonardo *(lay o nahr' doe)* German origin. Composed of the elements of *lewo* (lion) and *hart* (bold, strong, brave): hence the name means strong as a lion or lion bold. Prisoners and women in childbirth invoke Leonardo because of a wonderful tale. One day King Clovis and his wife were riding through the forest when she went into a terrible and difficult labor. Leonardo gave them shelter and delivered the baby. It is also believed his prayers saved the lives of both woman and child. A grateful Clovis granted him as much land as he could ride around by burro in one night. Leonardo established a monastery on the property and took in pardoned prisoners and returning crusaders. It may also be true that this saint's link to imprisonment may arise from the similarity of his name to *lien,* the French word for fetter.

Leoncio *(lay own' see oh)* Latin origin. Derived from *leo* (lion). Diminutive: Loncho. Variation: Leonicio.

Leopardo *(lay oh par' doe)* Latin origin. The name means leopard.

Liberato *(lee bay rah' toe)* Latin origin. Derived from Liberatus (he who has been liberated), which has its roots in *liberatus* (released, liberated). Variation: Librao.

Liduvino *(lee doo bee' no)* Teutonic origin. The name means he is a loyal friend.

Lisandro *(lee sahn' dro)* Greek origin. Derived from Lysandros (rescuer, liberator), which is composed of the elements *lysis* (loosening, releasing) and *andros* (man). Diminutives: Chando, Licho. Variation: Lisandrus.

Lobo *(lo' bo)* Latin origin. The name means wolf. According to Native American ideology the wolf is known as the pathfinder. He is the forerunner who forges ahead of the pack and brings back valuable information. He is a great teacher, is loyal, and mates for life. Wolf holds a strong connection to the moon, where all new ideas are just waiting to be called into manifestation. He howls at the moon, drawing out these wisdoms, which he later teaches to his people. Diminutive: Lobita.

Lorenzo *(low ren' zo)* Latin origin. Derived from Laurentius (of Laurentium), a name that has its roots in *laurus* (a laurel or bay tree). St. Lorenzo was a third-century martyr, one of the seven deacons of Rome, and is believed to rescue a soul from purgatory every Friday. When he was commanded to hand over all the wealth of the church he presented to the authorities hundreds of poor and handicapped people, widows, and orphans, proclaiming, "Here is the church's wealth." He was arrested and tortured but is said to have never lost his serenity and humor throughout the horrible agonies to which he was subjected.

Lucas *(loo' kahs)* Latin origin. Derived from Lucius (of Lucania), which has its roots in *lux* (light). St. Lucas was one of the apostles and known as Paul's "beloved physician." He is also characterized as being sympathetic toward women. He is the patron saint of painters due to the notion that he painted a portrait of the Virgin María, recounting the events of the nativity from memory.

Lucrecio *(loo cray' see oh)* Latin origin. The name means to gain wealth. Diminutive: Lulu. Variation: Lucresio.

Luis *(loo ees')* German origin. A cognate of the French Louis, a name that is derived from the German Hluodowig, which has its roots in the combination of the components *hloud* (famous, glorius) and *wīg* (war, battle): hence the name means famous in war or glorious battle.

Macario *(mah kah' ree oh)* Greek origin. Derived from *makaros* (blessed or fortunate one).

Macedonio *(mah say doe' nee oh)* Greek origin. The name means he who is enhanced through victories. Several saints were bestowed with this name. Variation: Macedonea.

Malaquías *(mah lah kee' ahs)* Hebrew origin. Derived from *mal'ākhī* (messenger or angel). Malaquís was the last prophet. In the Bible, it is the last book of the Old Testament. Variation: Malachinas.

Manasés *(mah nah sase')* Greek origin. Derived from *měnasse* (causing to forget). In the Bible a man by this name was the brother of Ephraim, son of Joseph and Asenath.

Manuel *(mahn well')* Hebrew origin. Derived from the Greek Emmanouēl, a name that has its roots in the Hebrew *immānūēl* (God is with us). According to the

Bible this name means a decendant of David, therefore
it signifies the Messiah.

Marcelino *(mar say lee' no)* Latin origin. Although it
is derived from Marcus (of Mars or warlike) it is bestowed as a separate name from Marcos. Mars, the Roman god of war, is also the namesake for the month
of March. The name appears sixty-nine times in the
Dictionary of Saints. Diminutive: Chelo. Variation:
Marselo.

Marcos *(mar' koze)* Latin origin. Derived from Marcus
(of Mars or warlike). Mars was the Roman god of war.
Another source states the name means hammer. Still
others believe it derives from *mas* (manly) or the Greek
malakoz (gentle, tender). Marcos was one of the apostles. St. Marcos's association with a winged lion may
derive from the fact that he abandoned his first mission
and possibly fled from the soldiers in the garden on
that fateful night. In the end he conquered his courage
and is credited with writing the first gospel, which
some say derive from Peter's teaching and serves as a
memoir. Variations: Marco, Marcus.

Marino *(mah ree' no)* Latin origin. Derived from Marinus (a man of the sea or a mariner). Of the thirty-
seven saints bestowed with this name the most beloved
was a saint from San Marino, Italy. He was a mason
and revered as a comforter of Christians.

Mario *(mar' ee oh)* Latin origin. Derived from Marcos,
the name means descending from Mars, the war god.
The name appears eleven times in the *Dictionary of
Saints*.

Martín *(mar teen')* Latin origin. Still another name bestowed as a stand-alone given name that is derived
from Marcos, the name means descending from Mars,
the war god. There have been forty saints bestowed
with this name, including one we can invoke against

drunkenness. Diminutive: Marto. Variation: Martini-
ano.

Mateo *(mah tay' oh)* Hebrew origin. Derived from Mat-
tathias, a name that has its roots in *mattīthyāh* (gift of
Yahweh, gift of God). Mateo was a tax collector, de-
spised by Jews and Gentiles alike, before he became
an apostle of Christ. Because of his economic back-
ground we can invoke this saint for issues regarding
money. The book of Matthew, the English equivalent
to Mateo, is the first of the Bible's New Testament.
Diminutive: Teo. Variation: Matheo.

Matías *(mah tee' ahs)* Greek origin. Hebrew origin. Derived from the Greek Matthias, which has its roots in
mattīthyāh (gift of Yahweh, gift of God).

Mauricio *(mau ree' see oh)* Latin origin. Derived from
Mauritius (Moor). The Moors were a Moslem people
of mixed Arab and Berber descent who lived in north-
western Africa.

Maximiano *(mahks ee mee ah' no)* Latin origin. The
name means son of Maximus, a name that literally signifies the greatest.

Maximiliano *(mahks ee mee lee ah' no)* Latin origin.
Compound of two Latin names: Maximus (the greatest)
and Aemmiliānus, a name that has its roots in *aemulus*
(emulating, trying to be like another): hence the name
means emulating the greatest. Seven saints bore this
name. Diminutive: Mancho. Variation: Mascimiliano.

Máximo *(mahks' ee mo)* Latin origin. Derived from
Maximus, a name that literally translates to mean the
greatest. Diminutive: Max. Variation: Másimio.

Melcor *(mel chor')* Hebrew origin. The name means
king of light. One of the Three Wise Men who brought
gifts for the Christ child on the night of his birth bore
this name.

Melesio *(may lay' see oh)* Greek origin. Derived from Meletios (careful, alert). Nine saints were bestowed with this name.

Mercurio *(mare coo' ree oh)* Latin origin. The name means he who takes care of business. Mercury is the Roman god of commerce and business. It is also the name of the planet closest to the sun. Mercury rules communications, including talking, writing, and teaching.

Miguel *(mee gell')* Hebrew origin. Derived from *mīkhā'ēl* (who is like God). Miguel the Archangel is the leader of the army of good who battle with Satan and evil. The reason for his patronage of grocers is based upon his task of receiving risen souls and weighing them in his scales. Diminutive: Mico.

Modesto *(mo dase' toe)* Latin origin. Derived from *modestus* (modest, down-to-earth, humble). Twenty saints bore this name.

Moisés *(moy sase')* Hebrew and Egyptian origin. Derived from the Hebrew Moshe, which has its roots in *mōsheh* (drawn out of the water) and the Egyptian *mes, mesu* (child, son): hence the name means "son drawn out of the water" or "because I drew him out of the water." In the Bible, he was the leader who parted the Red Sea, guiding the Israelites out of slavery in Egypt. On Mount Sinai he received the Ten Commandments and later led his people to the Promised Land.

Napoleón *(nah po lay own')* Greek origin. The name combines the elements *neapolis* (new city) with *león* (lion): hence the name means the lion of the new city.

Nathaniel *(nah than yell')* Hebrew origin. Derived from *nĕthan'ēl*, the name means gift of God.

Nazario *(nah aah' ree oh)* Hebrew origin. Derived from the Latin Nazaraeus, which comes from the Greek Nazaraios, a name that has its roots in *nāzir* (consecrated, sanctified). The name refers to a Nazarite, a person who voluntarily adheres to austere religious vows, hence the name has come to mean consecrated to God.

Néstor *(nase' tor)* Greek origin. The name means he remembers. The name was borne by a sagacious old counselor who fought with the Greeks at Troy.

Nicandro *(nee kahn' dro)* Greek origin. Composed of the elements *nikē* (victory) and *andros* (man): hence the name means the man of victory. The name was borne by nine saints, including a third-century Egyptian doctor martyred for ministering to Christians.

Nicolás *(nee co lahs')* Greek origin. Composed of the elements *nikē* (victory) and *laos* (people): hence the name means victory of the people or he who brings victory for his people. In the Bible, he was a follower of Jesus and one of the seven assistants to Christ's disciples. Nicolás of Myra became the popular St. Claus, patron saint of children and anonymous bringer of gifts. It is said he rescued three sisters from spinsterhood by giving them three bags of gold, saved three unjustly condemned men from death, rescued three sailors from drowning, and brought three boys back to life.

Nicomedes *(nee co may' days)* Greek origin. Composed of the elements *nikē* (victory) and *mēdesthai* (to meditate or contemplate): hence the name means he who contemplates victory.

Nuncio *(noon' see oh)* Latin origin. Derived from *nuntius* (announcer, messenger): hence the name has come to mean he who delivers a message or announcement.

Octavio *(oak tah' bee oh)* Latin origin. Derived from Octavius, a name that has its roots in *octavus* (eighth).

The name appears eight times in the *Dictionary of Saints*.

Omar *(oh mar')* Arabic origin. The name means builder.

Onésimo *(owe nay' see mo)* Greek origin. The name means that which is valuable, useful, and advantageous.

Onofre *(owe no' fray)* Teutonic origin. The name means defender of peace. Five saints bore this name, including a fourth-century hermit known as the patron saint of weavers. Variation: Onofrio.

Oscar *(oh scar')* Anglo-Saxon origin. The name is a combination of the elements *os* (a god, godliness, or goodness) and *gar* (spear): hence the name means possessing the spear of the gods, or the power of goodness.

Osmundo *(ohs moon' doe)* Anglo-Saxon origin. Compound of *os* (a god, divinity) and *mund* (hand or protection): hence the name means divine protection.

Osvaldo *(ohs ball' doe)* Anglo-Saxon origin. The name is an arrangement of *os* (a god, divinity, righteousness) and *weald* (power): hence the name means the power of God.

Pablo *(pah' blow)* Latin origin. Although it is a variation of Paulo, Pablo is often bestowed as a separate given name. It is derived from *paulus* (small). Diminutive: Pablino. Variation: Pavlo.

Paciano *(pah see ah' no)* Latin origin. Related to the Latin Pacianus (peaceful), which is derived from the word *pax* (peace). A fourth-century Spanish bishop bore this name. He was the author of theological treatises.

Pacífico *(pah see' fee ko)* Latin origin. This name is derived from the Latin *pacificare* (to pacify or appease, make peaceful), which has its roots in the word *pax* (peace): hence this name has come to mean he who makes peace. Diminutive: Paco.

Pascual *(pahs kwall')* Hebrew origin. Derived from the Latin Paschālis (of Easter), which comes from Pascha (Easter), a word that has its roots in the Hebrew *pesach* (Passover). The name is customarily given to a child born during the Easter or Passover season. Diminutives: Paco, Pasco. Variations: Pascuelo, Pazcual.

Patricio *(pah tree' see oh)* Latin origin. Derived from *patricius* (a patrician, a nobleman). Diminutives: Richi, Pachi. Variation: Patrizio.

Paulo *(pow' lo)* Latin origin. Derived from the Roman surname Paulus, which has its roots in *paulus* (small). It is also believed to be the Greek version of Saul, meaning "asked for." The Acts of the Apostles, from the Bible, is considered to be a compilation of the deeds and activities of Paulo. Paulo traveled far and wide to bring the gospel to the Gentile people. He is invoked for assistance with snakebites because of a legend that says a viper bit him on the hand but caused no harm. Diminutive: Pauli. Variation: Pauliciano.

Pedro *(pay' dro)* Aramaic origin. Greek translation of the Aramaic *cephas* (rock). St. Pedro is considered the foundation of the Christian church primarily because of Christ's trust in his first apostle and proclamation, "You are Pedro, and on this rock I build my church" (Matt. 16:18). Although he was one of the inner three prominent disciples (with John and James), he alone would be given the key to heaven. Diminutive: Pico. Variations: Petros, Piedro.

Pío *(pee' oh)* Latin origin. The name means pious, dutiful, and virtuous. The name was born by a twentieth-century mystic saint who bore the stigmata. He was of the Franciscan order and lived a life in accord with the example set forth by Jesus Christ.

Plácido *(plah' se doe)* Latin origin. Derived from *placidus* (placid, tranquil, peaceful, serene). Diminutive: Plasio. Variation: Plásido.

Porfirio *(pore fee' ree oh)* Greek origin. The name means he who is dressed in purple. Purple has long been the color of royalty. Variation: Porfiric.

Procopio *(pro ko' pee oh)* Greek origin. Derived from Prokopios, a name that has its roots in the arrangement of *pro* (before, preceeding) and *kopios* (copious, bountiful): hence the name means he who progresses with great wealth.

Próspero *(prose' pay ro)* Spanish origin. Derived from *próspero,* the name means prosperous.

Querido *(kay ree' doe)* Spanish origin. The name means to love. Modern translation signifies that a child bestowed with this name is beloved.

Querubín *(kay roo bean')* Hebrew origin. The name means cherub. Cherubs are angels, second closest to God. They are usually depicted as chubby childlike beings, often surrounding children, lovers, or women.

Quinto *(keen' toe)* Latin origin. Derived from *quintus* (fifth). Forty-two saints bore this name.

Rafael *(rah fah ell')* Hebrew origin. Derived from *refāēl* (God has healed). According to the Bible, in addition to being an archangel he was considered to be the temple gatekeeper. Diminutives: Falo, Rafi, Rafito. Variations: Rafaelo, Raphel.

Raimundo *(rye moon' doe)* German origin. Derived from the elements *ragin* (guidance, wisdom) and *mund* (protection, defense): hence the name means strong or wise defense. St. Raimundo is revered as a philan-

thropic saint who paid a great deal of his own money
as ransom for the deliverance of prisoners. When his
money ran out he offered his freedom so that one more
man could be freed. It is said a padlock was put
through his lips so he could no longer preach to the
prisoners. Diminutive: Mundo. Variations: Ramón, Ra-
mone, Reimundo.

Ramiro *(rah mee' roe)* Teutonic origin. The name
means powerful in the army. In the sixteenth century
it was customary for children to receive a surname that
was an adaptation of their father's first name. The popular surname Ramirez received its roots from this given
name approximately five hundred years ago.

Raúl *(rah ool')* Anglo-Saxon. The name is a combination of the elements *rath* (counsel) and *ulfr* (wolf):
hence the name means wolf counsel.

Refugio *(ray foo' hee oh)* Latin origin. The name means
refuge, safe haven. The name is given in honor of the
safety found in the Blessed Mother, hence Nuestra Señora del Refugio, Our Lady of Refuge. Diminutives:
Cuco, Refugito. Variations: Refugio, Refutio.

Reinaldo *(ray nahl' doe)* Teutonic origin. The name is
derived from a combination of the elements *ragna*
(judgment, counsel) and *walden* (to wield or rule):
hence the name means he who rules with good judgment. Diminutive: Naldo. Variations: Reginaldo, Ri-
naldo.

Remedio *(ray may' dee oh)* Latin origin. The name
means remedy, that which heals or cures, yet another
aspect of the Virgin María. Several churches adapt this
quality of the Blessed Mother for the name of their
church, such as Nuestra Señora de los Remedios (Our
Lady of Remedies). One such church in Mexico displays an image of the Virgin María brought from Spain
during the conquest.

Renato *(ray nah' toe)* Latin origin. Derived from Renātus, name that has its roots in the combination of *re* (again, anew) and *nātus* (born): hence the name means reborn. The name is often given as a baptismal name in honor of the person's spiritual rebirth under the watchful and loving eyes of God.

René *(ray nay')* Latin origin. Also derived from Renātus, which results from the combination of *re* (again, anew) and *nātus* (born): hence the name means reborn or born again.

Reyes *(ray' yays)* Latin origin. The name means king. A child bestowed with this name is in reference to the three kings who presented gifts to the Christ child on the night of his birth. It may also refer to the adoration, reverence, and humility they showed upon seeing the Christ child, which was particularly impressive to the common people, given their kingly status.

Ricardo *(ree kar' doe)* Anglo-Saxon origin. The name combines the elements of *rik* (ruler, king) and *hart* (strong, brave): hence the name means a strong ruler or brave king. There are nineteen saints with this name mentioned in the *Dictionary of Saints*. In the middle ages, St. Ricardo of Chichester did the unthinkable and most embarrassing act: he dropped the chalice during Mass. The great miracle and reason for the chalice being depicted with this saint is that he did not spill a drop of the consecrated wine. Diminutives: Cardo, Ricky, Rico. Variations: Rechard, Ricarrdo, Riqui.

Roberto *(ro bare' toe)* German origin. The name is an arrangement of the elements *hroud* (fame) and *beraht* (bright, brilliant): hence the name means brilliant with fame. Diminutives: Berto, Beto, Tito. Variation: Ruberto.

Rodolfo *(roe dole' foe)* German origin. The name combines the elements *hroud* (fame) and *wulf* (wolf):

hence the name means famous wolf. Diminutives:
Rolo, Rudi. Variations: Rodolpo, Rudulfo.

Rodrigo *(ro dree' go)* German origin. The name combines the elements *hroud* (fame, reputation) and *rik*
(ruler, king): hence the name means he who rules by
his reputation or famous ruler. Diminutive: Rod.

Rogelio *(roe hay' lee oh)* Teutonic origin. Derived from
the elements *hroud* (fame, glory) and *ger* (spear):
hence the name means he who knows glory or fame
by the spear. Six saints bore this name, including a
thirteenth-century disciple of St. Francis de Asís. Diminutive: Rugenio. Variations: Rogelia, Rogerio.

Rolando *(ro lahn' doe)* German origin. The name is a
combination of *hroud* (fame, glory) and *land* (land):
hence the name means fame of the land or glorious
land. Diminutives: Lando, Olo. Variations: Orlando,
Rolán.

Román *(ro mahn')* Latin origin. Derived from Romanus
(of or from Rome, the capital of Italy).

Rubén *(roo bane')* Hebrew origin. Derived from
rĕ'ūbēn (behold, a son!). In the Bible the name was
born by the first child of Jacob and Leah. He also became a patriarch of one of the twelve tribes. Variation:
Rubén.

Sacramento *(sah crah main' toe)* Latin origin. Derived
from *sacramentum* (sacrament, an oath of allegiance),
which has its roots in *sacer* (sacred, holy). It is also
the roots of several surnames such as Santos, Sánchez,
Sáenz, Saíz, and Sais.

Salomón *(sah low moan')* Hebrew origin. Derived from
shĕlōmōh (peaceful) a word that has its roots in *shālōm*
(peace). In the Bible the name was borne by King David's successor, who was known for his insightful wis-

dom and ability to communicate with animals. Diminutive: Moñi. Variation: Solomone.

Salvador *(sahl bah dor')* Latin origin. The name means savior, rescuer, and liberator. The name is bestowed in honor of Jesus Christ's sacrifice for the salvation of humankind. Diminutive: Chavo. Variations: Salbador, Salvadro.

Samuel *(sahm well')* Hebrew origin. Derived from *shĕmū'ēl* (his name is God). In the Bible, he was a judge and a prophet who anointed King Saul as the first king of Israel. Diminutives: Mel, Sami. Variation: Sameulo.

Sancho *(sahn' cho)* Latin origin. Derived from *sanctius* (sacred or holy).

Santiago *(sahn tee ah' go)* Latin origin. The name is composed of the elements *san* (saint) and Diego (a pet form of Jaime): hence the name means St. Jaime. Diminutive: Chango. Variations: Sandiego, Santava.

Saturnino *(sah toor nee' no)* Latin origin. Derived from Saturnus, the Roman god of agriculture, hence the name means protector of crops. It is also the namesake for Saturday and the planet Saturn. Saturn is the second largest planet in our solar system. Saturn's function is to aid us in the development of self-discipline, self-respect, and faith in one's destiny. The name appears eighty-four times in the *Dictionary of Saints*. Diminutives: Nino, Sasá. Variations: Satarino, Saturno, Saturnio.

Saúl *(sah ool')* Hebrew origin. Derived from *shāūl* (borrowed, asked for, longed for). In the Bible, he was the first king of Israel, from the tribe of Benjamin.

Sebastián *(say bahs tee ahn')* Greek origin. The name means worthy of adoration. The name appears fifteen times in the *Dictionary of Saints.* Diminutives: Chabo, Tano. Variations: Sevastián, Sebastín.

Segundino *(say' goon dee' no)* Latin origin. The name means following or second. The name is traditionally bestowed upon the second child. Variations of this name appear eighty-one times in the *Dictionary of Saints.* Variations: Seconideo, Secundio, Secundius.

Serafín *(say rah feen')* Hebrew origin. Derived from *sĕrāphīm* (seraphim, the burning one, or angels who surround God's throne), a word that has its roots in *sāraph* (to burn).

Sergio *(sare' hee oh)* Latin origin. The name means he who shepherds and protects. Thirty-three saints bore this name.

Servacio *(sare bah' see oh)* Latin origin. Derived from *servare* (to save, safeguard). Variation: Cerasio.

Severo *(say bay' ro)* Latin origin. Derived from the Roman surname of Sevērus (severe, austere, stern). The name was borne by fifty-one saints. Diminutive: Severito. Variations: Severano, Sivero.

Silvano *(seel bah' no)* Latin origin. Derived from the surname Silvānus (of the woods), a name that has its roots in *silva* (woods, forest). Also related to Sylvanus, the Roman god of fields, woods, and forests. Of the forty-two saints who bore this name the best known was from Clairvaux, France. He was awarded with visions of heaven. Variations: Silbano, Silviano.

Silvestre *(seel base' tray)* Latin origin. Derived from *silva* (woods or forest), the name means he who abides in the forest. Thirteen saints bore this name. Diminutive: Veche. Variations: Selvestre, Silvester, Sylbestrio.

Simón *(see moan')* Hebrew origin. Derived from *shim'ōn* (God has heard or to hear or be heard). From the Greek translation the name means snub-nosed. It was the given name of St. Pedro. The name appears fifty-one times in the *Dictionary of Saints*.

Sixto *(seeks' toe)* Latin origin. The name means sixth and is often bestowed upon the sixth child. Seven saints and three popes bore this name. Variations: Cisto, Sesto, Sixtio.

Teodoro *(tay o doe' ro)* Greek origin. The name is a combination of *theos* (God) and *dōron* (gift): hence the name means gift of God. One hundred and forty-six saints bore this name. Diminutives: Doro, Tedi. Variations: Teodario, Theador, Tieodoro.

Teodosio *(tay o doe' see oh)* Greek origin. The name means like a gift of God, and although similar to Teodoro and close to the same meaning, this name is often bestowed as a separate given name. Thirty-four saints were mentioned in the *Dictionary of Saints*. Diminutive: Teodos. Variation: Tiodoso.

Teófilo *(tay o' fee lo)* Greek origin. The name is a combination of *theos* (God) and *philos* (loving): hence the name means God's beloved. The name appears forty-seven times in the *Dictionary of Saints*.

Timoteo *(tee mo tay' oh)* Greek origin. Derived from a combination of the elements of *timē* (honor, respect) and *theos* (god): hence the name means he who honors God or respects God. In the Bible, a disciple and companion of Pablo.

Tito *(tee' toe)* Greek origin. Derived from *tío* (to honor). It is also believed to have come from the Latin Titus (safe). Although this name is often a diminutive it is also bestowed as a separate given name.

Tobías *(toe bee' ahs)* Hebrew origin. The name means God is good.

Tomás *(toe' mahs)* Aramaic origin. Derived from *tĕ'ōma* (a twin). Tomás, an apostle, is remembered as

Doubting Tomás because he refused to believe in the risen Christ until he touched his wounds. When the dawn of belief and faith came over him he proclaimed, "My Lord and my God!" (John 20:28), which has since become a powerful meditation prayer. Tomás is the patron saint of architects because of a characteristic legend of his life and disposition. Tomás was granted a large sum of money to construct a palace, for which he had the plans. Instead, Tomás symbolically built "a palace in heaven" by spending the money on the poor. Eighty-one saints bore this name. Diminutives: Max, Tomito. Variations: Tamascio, Tomaz.

Tránsito *(trahn' see toe)* Latin origin. The name means transfer, passage. The name is given in honor of the Virgin María and her passage onto heaven after her death. Diminutive: Tacho. Variation: Tráncito.

Trinidad *(tree nee dahd')* Latin origin. The name means trinity, which symbolizes the concept behind the central doctrine of Catholicism. The Trinity represents the three persons of God: the Father, Son, and Holy Spirit.

Tristán *(trees tahn')* Latin origin. The name means he who is God.

Tulio *(too' lee oh)* Latin origin. The name means risen from the ground.

Urbano *(oor bah' no)* Latin origin. The name means he who is courteous. It also is related to Urbānus (urban or city dweller). The name was borne by thirty saints and eight popes.

Valentín *(bahl en teen')* Latin origin. Derived from *valens* (strong, vigorous). Of the fifty-one saints who bore this name the one most remembered was St. Valentine, patron saint of love and medicine, whose feast day is February 14. Valentine was a Christian who tended the sick with herbs. It is believed he cured a young girl of blindness. Birds are said to pair on his feast day and combining this with the Roman feast of Lupercalia. St. Valentine became associated with choosing a mate and sending love letters. Diminutives: Tino, Val. Variations: Valante, Valentino, Valentío.

Valerio *(abh lair' ee oh)* Latin origin. Derived from *valere* (valiant, brave). The name was borne by thirty-nine saints and one bishop.

Venceslao *(bane sase lah' oh)* Slavic origin. Derived in part from the element of *slav* (glory), the name means he who is crowned with glory. Today he is remembered in the popular Christmas carol "Good King Wenseslas." The song speaks of a meeting between page and saint in which the page can no longer bear the brutalities of the winter's rage. The good king and saint walked in front of the young lad, providing protection, and miraculously it seemed as if "heat was in the very sod that the saint lay dinted." The message is that if we follow the goodness of saints and God we will find security and shelter from life's hardships. There are over sixty variations of this name, some of which are: Benceslado, Venesloa, Wencelaus, Wenseslas.

Venturo *(bane too' ro)* Latin origin. Derived from *ventura* (good fortune or good luck). Variations: Ventureno.

Víctor *(beak' tor)* Latin origin. The name means victor, champion, conqueror. The name appears 230 times in the *Dictionary of Saints.* Diminutives: Torico, Vito. Variations: Victoriano, Vittorio.

Vidal *(bee doll')* Latin origin. Derived from *vitalis* (vitality, full of life), a word that has its roots in *vita* (life). Fifty-two saints bore this name. Diminutive: Vita. Variations: Vidalo, Vitalis.

Vincentio *(bean sane' tee oh)* Latin origin. Derived from *vincere* (to conquer). Babies given this name often derive their name from Vincente de Paul. St. Vincente was highly dedicated to relieving human suffering and honored for his charitable endeavors. His life was a measure of extremes; he worked with people of great wealth and those condemned to a life of poverty. Such was his compassion that at one point he even took the place of a galley slave, which ruined his own health, so that the prisoner could be reunited with his family. Diminutive: Chenche. Variations: Biscente, Vicentino.

Xipto *(seep' toe)* Aztec origin. He was the Mexican god of silversmiths.

Zacarías *(zah kah ree' ahs)* Hebrew origin. Derived from *zĕcharyah* (God remembers). The name was borne by forty-two saints. In the Bible, he was the husband of Elizabeth and father of Juan the Baptist.

Zenobio *(zay no' bee oh)* Greek origin. The name is a combination of the elements *zēn* (Zeus) and *bios* (life): hence the name means the life of Zeus.

Zenón *(zay none')* Greek origin. Related to *zēn* (life), the name has come to mean the lively one or full of life. Variations: Semón, Zenén.